~UNDERWATER PARADISE~

A GUIDE TO THE WORLD'S BEST DIVING SITES
THROUGH THE LENSES OF THE
FOREMOST UNDERWATER PHOTOGRAPHERS

BY ROBERT BOYE

PHOTOGRAPHIC COORDINATION BY
THE WATERHOUSE INC.-BARBARA DOERNBACH

PHOTOGRAPHS BY:

STEPHEN FRINK
PAUL HUMANN
GERI MURPHY
CHRIS NEWBERT
CARL ROESSLER
MARTY SNYDERMAN
VALERIE TAYLOR
PAUL TZIMOULIS

HARRY N. ABRAMS, INC. • PUBLISHERS • NEW YORK

Editorial note:
The photographs in each section of the book are by the
photographer who has written the Vignette for that section.
Photographs by anyone else are credited in the captions.

CONTENTS

FOREWORD

DESCRIBING the world's best diving sites is an exercise in superlatives. Yet, that is the challenge we have undertaken for scuba divers: to describe the highest degree of experience in our sport.

While we have excluded most of the familiar, readily accessible, and therefore heavily dived sites, we have tempered our selection process with a degree of practicality. Our criteria for choice of dive destinations are straight-forward:

1. That the book's contributors would desire to revisit the locale
2. That the environment has one or more features or conditions that make it unique
3. That support services are both reliable and safe
4. That the destination is accessible through normal means of transportation
5. That the site itself has an ambiance that sets it apart.

In our judgment, each chapter presents one of the best diving locales in the world. Although each is not necessarily the most exotic of its kind, some certainly are. All, however, are unique in some way. Since cost is a factor that few can ignore, we have chosen some locations within easy reach of the United States. (The seaweed really isn't greener on the other side of the international dateline.) Yet, each of these destinations has a special aura about it.

We have refrained from cataloging or recommending specific diving facilities or operators. Other resources are available for that purpose. Experience has taught us that businesses and their personnel are far more transient than the conditions of the sites themselves. Therefore, we urge you to do your homework carefully before committing time and money to a trip. Seek first-person evaluations: reputable dive resorts and specialized travel agencies will gladly provide the names of people who have been recent customers. Contact them and ask your own questions.

When you have dived at one or more of these locations, we feel certain that your perspective and outlook on diving will change. Having seen and experienced the best, you will never again be satisfied with the mundane. Happy and safe diving!

**CLARK'S ANEMONEFISH SHOW extremely varied coloration; their basic colors can range from orange to black.
(Chris Newbert)**

7

Opposite:
PHOTOGRAPH BY VALERIE TAYLOR.

Preceding pages:
**NOT MORE THAN HALF AN INCH long, this juvenile fish seeks the protection of bubble coral.
(Chris Newbert)**

INTRODUCTION
TO THE WORLD'S BEST DIVING SITES

WHEN SOME OF THE WORLD'S foremost underwater photographers were asked to identify what one question was most frequently put to them by divers, their answer was, "Where is your favorite dive site?" This question isn't surprising given the tremendous growth in international dive travel during the past ten years. Sport divers want to see those places where professional photographers choose to perform their craft. And it is usual in this sport to rely upon word-of-mouth recommendations when choosing dive destinations.

What may be surprising, however, is the variety of responses to the question. Further, our contributors invariably qualified their answers, asserting that some places are clearly better than others — for some things. It all depends upon what you're looking for, how much time and/or money you have, and when you can travel.

We have compiled the collective opinions of a group of professional underwater photographers. Our choices are represented by images captured through their camera lenses. We hope that our consensus assures the reader a reasonable degree of objectivity. Our goal has simply been to select the best diving sites in the world and to show through pictures, facts, and forthright opinions why we chose them.

Opinions, of course, are by their very nature subjective. Furthermore, they may include debatable conclusions. We realize that some of ours may be considered harsh, but the alternative of strictly factual reporting strikes us as dull and perhaps misleading. We are not beholden to any tourist bureaus, chambers of commerce, airlines, or dive operators. Instead, we have frankly stated our likes and dislikes on all manner of subjects.

We have chosen to concentrate on an underwater photographic appraisal of diving locations. Our collective experience indicates that most divers are motivated by a sense of adventure and a strong desire to experience the natural beauty and wonderment afforded at various sites. To most, the "doing" is far more important than possessing an encyclopedic knowledge of marine biology. Thus, we have presupposed that you either already have a basic understanding or will acquire one elsewhere.

SLENDER-BODIED BARRACUDA
can reach a length of eight feet.
(Chris Newbert)

WHY WE CHOSE THESE SITES: THE ULTIMATE TEST

Perhaps the ultimate criterion of our international "wish list" is the desire of each of our contributors to return to these locations. For a variety of reasons, our appetites have not been sated.

UNIQUENESS

Each environment has something unique in its features or diving conditions, some obvious, others more subtle. For example, if you are attracted to shipwrecks, the thought of traveling to remote Truk Lagoon in Micronesia might seem ludicrous when so many wrecks are accessible from U.S. shores. Yet, nowhere else are there so many wrecks in such close proximity with such ideal diving conditions.

SUPPORT SERVICES

Both the reliability and safety of diver support services were a critical factor in the selection process. We excluded some areas of the world where, in our opinion, divers are at risk. Dependable delivery of services by trained operators is essential.

SPONGE AND PARROTFISH ON
the hull of the *Fujikawa Maru.*
(Geri Murphy)

ACCESSIBILITY

International air travel is both expensive and physically tiring. Couple with this the old adage that "the more remote the location, the better the diving" and you have a diver's paradox. Is truly great diving worth the hassle? We think the answer is yes — to a degree. This is why dealing with reputable dive travel operators is important. Before offering a trip to the public, they have visited the locales, checked accommodations, travel connections, and the myriad of other logistical details involved. While some travel requirements to reach our suggested sites may be lengthy or expensive, they are doable.

AMBIANCE

Finally, we have allowed ourselves the luxury of subjectivity. Based on our collective experience, we feel these locations possess an ambiance that sets them apart from dozens of others. Each of our contributors has logged dives by the thousands and air miles by the tens of thousands. Like long-haul truck drivers who congregate at only a few stops, we have tested the waters of the world and offer you our favorite places.

THE ROYAL ANGELFISH IS ONE of the most strikingly colored fishes found in the Red Sea. (Carl Roessler)

A WORD OF CAUTION

In spite of our best efforts to steer you to the right locations, man and nature can and do make a muddle of things occasionally. Plane flights can be delayed or cancelled. Military coups or civil unrest can occur. And too, Mother Nature can whip up unseasonal storms; or the creatures we are seeking, such as the manta rays in the Sea of Cortez, may not be at their favorite feeding grounds when your boat arrives.

BEST ADVICE

Given all the adverse things that can happen when you venture to some of the world's more remote locations, we strongly urge you to take ample supplies of three things: patience, flexibility, and a sense of humor. All will keep you in good stead.

SOME PRACTICAL ADVICE: GROUP TOURS VS. INDIVIDUAL TRAVEL

Some years back when my wife and I considered ourselves inexperienced divers, the thought of joining a group diving tour was farthest from our minds. One reason was an inferiority complex, a feeling that we weren't good enough to make it in the big leagues. Oddly enough, the other reason was a superiority complex, the belief that we were above being led around by a tour director. We were wrong on both counts. In hindsight, our biggest problem was our failure to differentiate between traditional vacations, which tend to

THE
RED SEA

When God, or Allah, created the Sinai, he left his paint palette home. The Book of Deuteronomy called it a "great and terrible wilderness." Whether you are flying from Cairo or Tel Aviv, it looks similar: harsh, rugged, arid, monochromatic, seemingly devoid of any vegetation, with the exception of the few oases. In short, the Sinai doesn't look like a nice place to live. It isn't and it never has been. Rain rarely falls there.

Life is in a constant struggle with the environment, both physical and political. Few places in the world can boast about so

sink) in the Dead Sea's viscous waters is an experience worth having – once.

Travelling to the Red Sea via Cairo is comparable in time required, but a different experience. Egypt's economy and standard of living are just edging into the twentieth century. The contrasts of old and new are dramatic. Most of the country's population is crowded into the arable land of the lower Nile River valley. Cairo is modernizing quickly, but the process involves almost constant traffic gridlock. Modern skyscrapers and apartment buildings straddle the Nile and have crept westward almost to the parking lots abutting the pyramids of Giza, where a group resembling the local Teamsters Union controls the camelride concessions. Egyptologists could spend a lifetime studying ancient history. For me, two days of sightseeing were interesting, but enough for a lifetime. Friends, however, have taken the opportunity to go up the Nile to the Temples of Luxor. They assure me that the grandeur observed is well worth the trip.

EPICUREAN DISMAY

And now a word about the food – *bad!* If Michelin rated dining in the Sinai, including the live-aboard boats, its pages would be like a starless night. The reality is not without reason. American palates are accustomed to an abundance of fresh produce, fruits, and meats, but Egypt's economy simply doesn't have a wide variety of foods, it being a Third World country with over

40-million mouths to feed and having an income per capita of less than five hundred dollars. In fact, the U.S. government, with more American employees in Egypt than in any other country in the world, is forced to satisfy its personnel's food demands itself. The Air Force supplies the American commissaries with weekly flights of a jumbo jet.

For live-aboard boats based out of Eilat, Israel, the food situation is different but not necessarily better. Food in Israel is governed mostly by religious laws and partially by availability. Thus, pork, beef, and lamb are not readily found. Chicken and turkey are popular and seafood would seem to be a natural, especially aboard a boat. But here we have another Red Sea paradox. Although the water teems with food fish, they are protected in most areas used by divers. Not only is spearfishing banned, all fishing is. During their most recent occupation of the Sinai, the Israelis protected most of the eastern and southern coastlines as conservation and wildlife areas for the benefit of divers and naturalists. When the Sinai was returned to Egypt in 1982, Egyptian authorities established the waters around the Sinai as that country's first national park. Thus, fresh fish can only be caught when a boat is well away from the coastline. But dive boats usually hug the shore.

The moral of the story is: "Don't go to the Red Sea for eating, go for the diving." You will be fed adequately, if not blandly. You may even learn to like camel and goat! Poultry is a staple. If you need Grape-Nuts for breakfast, bring them with you. For those who want more than coffee, tea, soft drinks, or Egyptian beer for beverages, we suggest bringing powdered concentrates. The oases provide pure and sweet-tasting water.

Another price of paradise is the lack of medical facilities. In an emergency, the nearest hospital is over a hundred miles away. There are no drug stores. In fact, there are few stores of any sort. So, bring any medications you might need with you.

Right:

BUMP-HEADED WRASSES CAN **easily attain five-foot lengths and weigh several hundred pounds. (Stephen Frink)**

Opposite, above:

MOST SPECTACULAR OF THE **Red Sea nudibranchs is the giant sea slug, commonly called Spanish dancer.**

Opposite, below:

WHAT APPEARS TO BE A SOFT **coral is actually a ribbonlike mass of nudibranch eggs attached to the reef.**

thias squamipinnis) perform their synchronized ballet along the reef walls. They aren't unique to the Red Sea, but they seem to be more abundant there. Darting, dancing, shifting, and sliding against the multicolored backdrop of the coral-encrusted reef, each school maintains its territory. Occasionally, thousands of these sparkling jewels can be seen cascading down a coral head in a waterfall of orange droplets.

Aside from the esthetic spectacle they create, these fish are a biological curiosity. Like many species they are all born hermaphroditic. Those that survive to maturity may breed as females for several years, existing in a harem dominated by one or more males, depending on the harem's size.

When the social opportunity presents itself, i.e., a male dies or simply disappears, a mature and usually dominant female will begin to develop into a male. While the process only takes a few days, the transformation is dramatic. A characteristically long spine begins to develop at the front of the dorsal fin; the fins lengthen. Simultaneously, the internal organs change from female gender to male. Within days the metamorphosis transforms an attractive scullery maid into a regal prince. Distinctly darker red tones predominate; royal violet spots appear on the pectoral and pelvic fins. His tail fins extend like an elegant cape and he assumes his position of dominance, crowned by

Opposite:
AT RAS MUHAMMAD, ANEMONES grow to gigantic sizes. (Stephen Frink)

WITH MOUTH OPEN AND GILLS flared, this coral grouper is being groomed of parasites at a "fish cleaning station."

the long, sweeping crest at the beginning of his dorsal fin.

The obvious question, then, is: from whence do the males come? The answer is a biological process known as "protogynous hermaphroditism," meaning, quite simply, "female first." For most jewelfish, however, their role is female always, for a school does not need many males to maintain itself.

Swirling Skirts

Certainly the most spectacular of the Red Sea nudibranchs (pronounced nude-e-brank and meaning "snail with naked gills") is the giant scarlet sea slug (*Hexabranchus sanguineus*), the Spanish dancer. This beautiful creature grows to a length of twelve to fourteen inches and is colored a deep red, with the exception of a thin, blue-white edge to the mantle and brilliant orange, feather-like gills on its back. When this nocturnal animal swims, by means of a series of wave-like undulations of its mantle from front to back, the waving edge of the body looks like the swirling skirts of a Spanish flamenco dancer. Indeed, to touch its vermillion skirt, one would be convinced the fabric was a richly textured velvet.

Spanish dancers are considered by many to be a prize photographic catch during a night dive. On one occasion, we found *three* dancers. On most night dives, we find none. Since they are nocturnal feeders, the key to discovery is to dive at night and find their favorite food, the soft coral *Sarcophyton*.

Anemone City

We all had seen other species of anemones and anemonefishes before, but these stoichactid sea anemones and fish (*Amphiprion bicinctus*) were incredible! Commonly called the two-banded anemonefish, they are endemic to the Red Sea. Normally, this specie's adults form permanent pair bonds; they are monogamous. Ordinarily, an adult pair will dominate its host anemone, tolerating the presence of one or two juveniles but also inhibiting their growth. Routinely, divers can expect to see one adult pair living in symbiotic harmony within, around, and darting about the hundreds of tentacles that the anemone uses to sting and kill like-sized fishes of other families. Somehow the anemonefish are immunized or acclimatized to the mortal stings. And in some way, their presence benefits the anemone, possibly by grooming it of parasites or by dropping tidbits of food into its waving tentacles.

Something about the particular location at Ras Muhammad, a site called "Anemone City," had nurtured anemones of gigantic proportion, like a science-fiction experiment gone berserk. In my frame of reference, a large anemone is the size of a bathmat, but these dozen or so matched the size of my front hall rug, perhaps four-by-six feet, but asymmetrical in shape with a long shag of tentacles. Nor did each shelter the usual two or three anemonefish, but rather ten or twelve adults. And they were in deeper water than that in which anemones are usually found, fifty-five to seventy-five feet. Draped like prayer rugs at rest on the steep reef face, some looked like miniature waterfalls. At that depth, the undersides of these creatures appeared to be a very dark, almost blackish, green. When exposed to the light of a strobe,

Opposite:
**MAP ANGELFISH ARE NAMED
for the bright yellow marking on
their sides that resembles the
shape of the African continent.**

A MALE JEWELFISH IS STRIKINGLY different in both markings and coloration from the female it used to be. (Robert Boye)

however, a brilliant red reflected instantly.

Most marine authors report that the anemonefish, a member of the damselfish family, is the only fish that can survive among the anemone's deadly stinging tentacles. Experts are sometimes wrong!

For in the Red Sea at Ras Muhammad, we first saw the sight which we have since confirmed at several other locations throughout the Indo-Pacific area. The anemonefish's cousin, the domino damselfish (*Dascyllus trimaculatus*), also maintains a symbiotic relationship with the sea anemone. Even more startling is that the cousins exist together peacefully. Normally the anemonefish shows aggressive behavior toward any fish (or diver) approaching its host. But at "Anemone City," the little black damselfish with two or three round white spots on its sides has succeeded at coexistence. In fact, those jumbo anemones literally had hundreds of domino damsels in and among their tentacles, all freely associating with the anemonefish. I can't help but fantasize that these usually belligerent creatures symbolize the peace between the Egyptians and Israelis.

AFTERTHOUGHTS

When diving in the Red Sea, especially for the first time, concentration is difficult. Literally thousands of animals compete for your attention. Capturing specific mental images becomes a challenge. These are but a few of mine, but they are representative of the beauty, oddity, diversity, and, above all, color found there. I could have written just as easily about the rare ghost pipe fish, the four species of endemic butterfly fishes, the bizarrely shaped and marked Picasso fish, the blinking lantern fish, or hundreds of others.

FRAGMENTS OF PARADISE— THE RED SEA

While we who take underwater photographs are fiercely proud of our work, I must confess that our very best photos are but a pale reflection of what you can encounter under the Red Sea. The spaciousness, intensity, and profusion of reef life, the majesty of sharks, rays, turtles, and other creatures—all are beyond our meager craft. All we can show you are isolated scenes, for it is impossible to convey the colossal reality going on simultaneously everywhere around us.

In a way, I am glad of that. For if we could convey in a mere book the kaleidoscopic wonder of the Red Sea, what motivation would you have to dream of your own adventure there? I have escorted many groups of divers there; I enjoy watching them be dazzled by unending visual spectaculars.

Between the Sinai and the Sudan lie some of the most remote, electric reefs on the planet, places only a handful of divers have ever seen. They have the eye-throbbing excitement of a canvas by Picasso, Miro, or Van Gogh. Over the years we have gradually widened the area in the Red Sea that divers can explore. In the 1970s, we were limited to the region around Sharm-el-Shiekh at the southern tip of the Sinai desert. Now we have extended our reach as far south as the Sudan, opening wondrous new sites for diving.

There are the soaring twin towers of Ras Muhammad, poised at the abyss like the abutments of a medieval castle; the remote pinnacles of Snaphir, lushly alive; the lagoon of Sha'ab Rumi, rich with history, the site of some of Jacques Cousteau's earliest public entertainments; and the monolithic lighthouse at Sanganeb Reef, brooding over what must be the best single dive site in the world.

Over the last twenty years I have been fortunate enough to lead most of the openings of major dive destinations around the world for avid American divers; my entire career has been spent advising divers as to what reef experiences would best suit their needs. The Red Sea has been one of my aces—I can always play it and win.

· LEMON BUTTERFLYFISH ARE FOUND ONLY IN THE RED SEA. ·

And, in my other career as a professional photojournalist, the Red Sea is still an ace. When I need a game-stopping card, I can count on the soft corals, the lemon butterflyfish, the sharks, the barracuda schools, the immense wrecks...

So, in the complex arena of a diver's fondest dreams, the Red Sea remains one of those "brass rings" to reach for, one whose memories tower over those of lesser places.

For this dreamer, there is the hope that someday politics will recede and that more divers will make their way to these paradise reefs. Why, I could tell you where....

VIGNETTE   BY   CARL   ROESSLER

THE
GREAT
BARRIER REEF

Australians boast about their number one tourist attraction the way Texans boast about their state. It is vast, encompassing an area of one hundred thousand square miles that spans fourteen degrees of latitude and ten degrees of longitude off the northeastern coast of the island continent. The Great Barrier Reef is great — the largest coral reef complex in the world. It is a barrier — with few deepwater, navigable passages in a length comparable to the U.S. shoreline between New York City and Miami, Florida.

But it is not a single reef! Rather, it is a galaxy

of separate reefs, perhaps twenty-five hundred in all. Some are small, house-sized "bommies." [In Australian jargon, any reef is a bommie, derived from the aborigine word *bombora,* or submerged rock.] Others are huge formations up to twenty square miles in area.

Regardless of their size, they all take one of four distinct forms. Some are *fringing* reefs, elongated structures lying parallel with and near the shore. Others are *barriers,* also elongated and more or less parallel with the shore but lying much further away. Sometimes, as in Australia, these become disjointed and much more complex in shape. The term *patch* reef is a catchall for a variety of small reefs that take the general form of a flat-topped hill. These are always simple in form, with sides sloping away in all directions, usually on a

Preceding pages:
A MONTAGE OF CUP CORALS
and tunicates.

FROM A DISTANCE, THIS
school of feather-fin bullfish
bears a resemblance to
moorish idols, which
rarely school.

comparatively shallow sea bed. No *atolls* appear in the Great Barrier Reef. However, a few are found outside it in the very deep waters of the Coral Sea. Viewed from above, they generally appear as more or less circular rings of coral enclosing a lagoon. Sometimes they surround the subsided volcanic island around which a reef originally formed. These Australian atolls are among the finest diving sites found anywhere.

Inside the Reef lies a protected, navigable channel that runs the entire length of the state of Queensland. It varies in width from about 10 miles at Cape Melville in the north to over 150 miles at the Swain Reefs in the south.

A Misunderstood Legacy

Of all the coral reef communities in the world, none contain as many species of life. Divers are bedazzled and bewildered by the array of algae, corals, fishes, crabs, starfish, molluscs, and other animal groups. The small reef area surrounding Heron Island, for example, located at the extreme southern end of the Reef off the coast of the city of Gladstone, is less than fourteen square miles. It has been studied intensively for over thirty years. The catalog of species identified is mind-boggling: 931 species of fish, 107 corals, 27 featherstars, 36 holothurians, 25 sea urchins, 32 brittle-stars. No one knows

HUMBUGS RARELY VENTURE FAR from the protection of the coral head where they live.

how many species of molluscs inhabit the area, but thirty-four species of cone shells alone have been identified. When you add soft corals, sponges, gorgonians, hydroids, anemones, worms, bryozoans, ascidians, and crustaceans, the cataloging task for this tiny area would require a host of researchers and a mainframe computer. (Ironically, Heron Island was converted to a tourist resort and marine research station in 1932 after the turtle canning industry had wiped out its primary resource and abandoned the site. Now marine biologists study ways to protect and rejuvenate the endangered sea turtle populations.)

Scientists, who rarely seem to agree on things unprovable, concur that the Reef's tropical location near the center of the vast Indo-Pacific basin together with its two-thousand-million year ecological history have contributed to its unique evolution.

The relatively shallow waters of the continental shelf, rarely exceeding thirty fathoms (180 feet), offer ideal conditions for the world's largest coral farm. The water is generally clear and warm. The slowly sinking shelf provides a hard substrate on which coral larvae can affix themselves. The water is usually well oxygenated. Finally, the shallow waters admit the adequate light required for coral growth.

Random dots of ocher appear on charts of the Great Barrier Reef. These are generally small, low-lying coral islets, some inhabited, some not. They are piles of sand and coral rubble swept up by the ocean's broom. A few support resort hotels and/or scientific laboratories. Others are protected bird rookeries. Some are densely vegetated, but none have significant reservoirs of fresh water.

Loosely enclosed within the Reef, generally near the coastline, lie four hundred-or-so splotches of rugged, rocky islands of granite or other igneous rocks. Once mainland mountain peaks, they were marooned when the Pacific Ocean's water level rose. Many are lushly carpeted with greenery and white sand beaches and adorned with luxury hotels. None are suitable for world-class scuba diving.

EYE TO EYE WITH A POISONOUS freckled porcupinefish.

GETTING THERE

Prior to 1980, foreign divers wishing to visit the Coral Sea and Far Northern Reefs were forced to fly into either Sydney or Melbourne, transfer to domestic

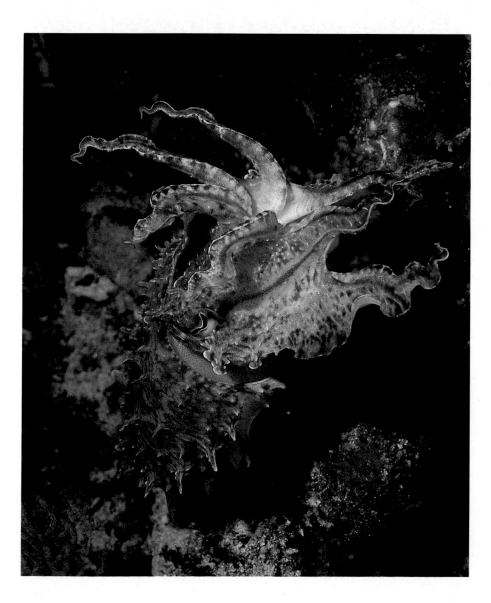

47

CUTTLEFISH ARE NORMALLY placid, but when agitated their distress is obvious.

THE GREAT BARRIER BOOMERANG

For many neophytes to international diving, the Great Barrier Reef is revered as the ultimate dive destination. Like young children awed by the hoopla of Christmas, they naively believe the barrage of marketing and promotional propaganda that has been bombarding them since the early 1980s. That was when the Australian Tourist Commission, Queensland Tourist and Travel Corporation, Qantas Airways, and Australian diving operators launched an all-out marketing campaign to attract divers and other tourists from North America and Japan. Who can forget Qantas's koala pictured with mask, snorkel, and flippers, the thirty-page special supplements in diving magazines, or the expensive, four-color brochures provided by Qantas and dive-tour operators? They were and are good for business, effective in attracting divers, but misleading for those, like me, who accepted them as gospel truth.

The glossy hype features superlatives battling for supremacy. But, apparently for the good of the multi-million-dollar tourist industry, they omit any reference to the realities of the Reef's actual condition, which has deteriorated markedly in the central two-thirds during the past twenty-five years. It is as if a world-class hotel let 80 percent of its rooms get seedy without reducing rates to compensate for threadbare carpets, torn drapes, and dirty windows. Guests would justifiably be angry and disappointed. And that is what has happened to so many divers who have not experienced the best of what the Great Barrier Reef and the Coral Sea offer.

Make no mistake about it, there is world-class diving in Australia — some of the very best. But to sample it, divers must be selective, willing to pay for a live-aboard boat, and willing to take the extra day or two required for travel to the northern reefs and/or the Coral Sea.

AN AQUEOUS WATERGATE

On our first trip in November 1983, we had chosen a live-aboard boat out of Townsville. My mind's eye had conjured up many images of the fabled Reef, from pounding surf to acres of exposed reef flats and even lush, coconut-studded honeymoon islets. Thus, I was surprised by the reality of the situation when I reached the inner edge. All I could see was water, nothing but water. Only its color signified the undersea topography. We entered a maze of mesa-like bommies, none of which broke the surface. Our first two days of diving were interesting, but not noteworthy.

We were all looking forward to our next destination, an overnight trip beyond the Reef's outer edge that would take us into the Coral Sea to the Flinders Reef atoll. The boat's captain and crew attempted to discourage us from making this leg of our cruise. They intimated that we would find the diving much better if we stayed within the reef complex. Frankly, we suspected their motives, thinking they merely wanted to conserve on fuel. After all, we had read an enthusiastic review of Flinders diving in the May edition of a well-known publication. Consequently, we persevered and endured that night's eighty-mile crossing through oceanic swells that left many seasick and others on the brink.

The two days of diving there rank high on my lifetime list of poor dives. Quite simply, the fifteen-mile lagoon had been decimated. We estimated that 80 percent of the coral was dead. No matter where we anchored, the destruction was the same. It was a ghost town of bleached coral skeletons covered with the slime of algae.

The American dive tour operator and the publication lost all credibility. Only the crew had been honest. What we saw had to have occurred years prior to our trip. Why we, the diving public, weren't told can only be a matter of cynical speculation. But while it was not included in any of the tourism ads, what has happened to the Great Barrier Reef is a matter of public record.

Crown-of-Thorns Starfish

Thirty years ago, the crown-of-thorns starfish (*Acanthaster planci*) was an oddity on the Reef, rarely found there or anywhere else. These gluttons are peculiarly well-adapted for what they do best — eating the polyps of hard corals. They are large, up to twenty-four inches across. They have many arms,

THE GIANT TRITON, ONE OF THE three known natural predators of the crown-of-thorns starfish, attacks its voracious prey.

its most tranquil. Occasionally, divers can stage the brutality of a shark feeding-frenzy. It is not for the weak at heart or inexperienced, because once a school of sharks runs amok, conditions are dangerous and unpredictable.

Anybody's adrenalin would flow at the sight of a dozen white-tipped torpedoes rocketing through the maze of speared fish we had tied to coral, buoyed up by empty plastic bottles. What began as cautious circling at minuette pace soon turned into a staccato frenzy of motion culminated by the gray blur of a beast smashing into the faceplate of my camera housing.

Occasionally, Moorish idols (*Zanclidae*), saucer-sized fish with dorsal pennants streaming, are seen in schools. Usually though, we have seen them in pairs, feeding on algae. Thus, I was amazed to see a shoal. Technically, since they aren't schooling fish, what I saw was an "aggregation" of fish, probably a gathering for the communal purpose of spawning. The visual impact was mind-blowing! Perhaps one hundred were marching back and forth in perfect formation like a football half-time spectacle. Each time they marched to the rear, their broad, slightly angled body stripes reversed their tilt, giving the optical effect of geometric patterns changing to waltz tempo.

My second dive to the *Yongala* was a mistake, almost a classic case in the exercise of poor judgment. What had been unusually bad conditions on the first dive had deteriorated even more. The wind was blowing harder, pushing the waves into higher peaks, deeper troughs, and also increasing the current's velocity. This combination roiled up the water; visibility was down to ten feet. Since it was impossible to swim against the current, above or below the surface, the crew had rigged a line from the stern dive platform that ran underneath the wildly pitching hull and attached it to the anchor line. Of course, we didn't know how much the current had increased and the visibility decreased until we got underwater.

Only four men were foolish enough to attempt this dive. To reach the wreck, we had to carefully time our leaps to coincide with the platform reaching its nadir, then immediately grab the guideline and pull ourselves under the boat until we got to the anchor line; from that point, we had to pull down the heavier hawser until we reached the ship's rail. By the time I reached the *Yongala*, I was breathing heavily from the exertion of fighting the waves and current. I had used a lot of air and knew I shouldn't be there. But the others, all younger by ten or fifteen years, forged ahead. I hesitated, then followed. But

A FEMALE LOGGERHEAD TUR-tle, **member of an endan-gered species.**

Opposite:
BLUE ANGELFISH ARE VERY **territorial and will harass any fishes with similar feeding habits.**

in that moment, I had lost sight of them *and* the anchor line.

I had already broken two of diving's cardinal rules: I should have aborted the dive as soon as I felt the first pangs of anxiety; failing to abort, I never should have become separated from my "buddy" (nor he from me). But I had done both and was alone in a dangerous situation. My anxiety turned to the real fear of running out of air. And that fear fed on itself to the point where I slipped into hyperventilation (excessively rapid and deep breathing that uses even more of a diver's limited quantity of compressed air). I bordered on the hysterical, irrational edge of full panic. I opted to go up to the boat — alone.

The line between fear and panic can't be seen, only experienced. Seconds of irrational thought and behavior that jolt the body into seemingly uncontrollable hyperventilation battle with training, experience, and logic. Panic was about to rout my sanity and safety on the most frightening dive of a lifetime.

As I dragged myself along the exposed rail, I realized I had passed the anchor line. Or had I? Should I go back or forward or just let go and surface in the fifteen foot swells and racing current? But no one would see me! I had no whistle to signal! Sucking air uncontrollably, I was disoriented and in serious trouble. Then, one sane thought, perhaps born from experience or training, entered my consciousness. "Stop! Get control over the hyperventilation. Force yourself to slow your breathing." It worked. Another twelve feet forward and the dim diagonal of the line appeared. Slowly, I climbed back to the wildly pitching boat. "Never again," I vowed. No photographs are worth those moments of fear. Never again will I choose to dive with all conditions negative or without a buddy.

THE GREAT BARRIER REEF'S FUTURE?

Twenty-five years ago, the Great Barrier Reef Committee, a group of distinguished scientists, shared a curious mind-set. They sincerely believed they could develop a master plan that would provide for both controlled conservation and exploitation for recreational purposes of the entire area. Their thinking was based on one underlying assumption — that it was possible to isolate one part of the Reef and exploit it without damaging other parts.

In 1975, the Australian government assumed the primary role of the Reef's protector by declaring the area a marine park and by establishing an authority to manage it and zone it for specific uses. In order to strike a balance between the conservationists and politicians, the Great Barrier Reef Marine Park Authority was empowered to provide for both preservation and recreation. With the efficiency of most bureaucracies, the Authority took ten years to bring the entire Reef under its aegis.

Thus far, recreation and tourism have received favorable treatment in the Authority's efforts to promote controlled exploitation while, at the same time, preserving the Reef for posterity. Meanwhile, in 1988 the world's first self-contained floating resort opened near Townsville. Anchored within the Reef, the resort features a seven-story hotel complete with marina, swimming pool, heliport, and tennis court. The Authority has assured anxious conservationists that this facility will not release any pollutants onto the Reef. All garbage, sewage, and man-made wastes will be barged back to the mainland, they say. No fuel leaks from diesel oil or gasoline barges will occur. Pool chemicals will never seep into the sea. Small boats will never exude the oil slicks found in marinas around the world. The noise and activity of hundreds of humans will not in any way disturb existing marine life. And the untested design will never break loose from its moorings during a cyclone. We can only hope that they are correct. For if they are wrong in their assurances, the Reef will suffer grievous damages.

This is the most recent ominous harbinger of the Reef's future and the government's oddly skewed concern for it. Hopefully, no dire events will occur. For the present, at least, divers should heed Valerie Taylor's words: "It really is the best in the world....It is just a matter of knowing where to go."

WHITETIP REEF SHARKS, USUALLY timid, avoid close encounters with divers.

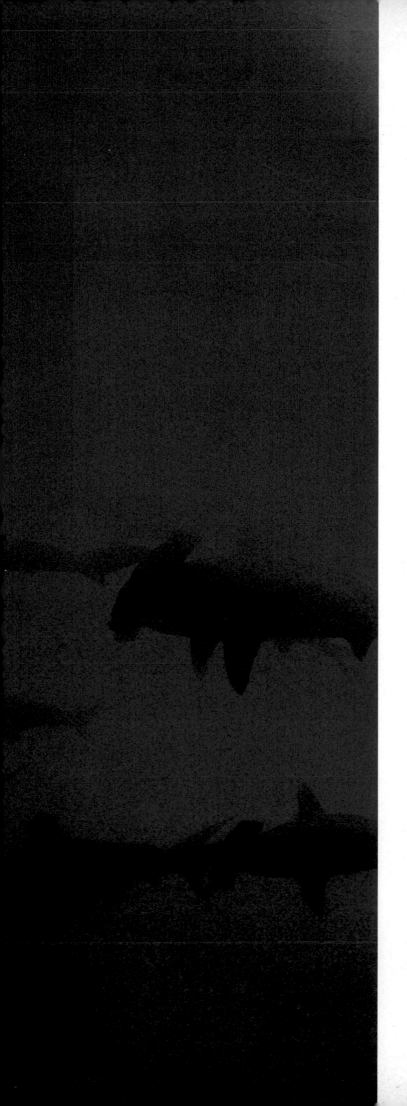

THE SEA OF CORTEZ
A COLOSSAL FISH TRAP

Twenty-five million years ago, Mexico was a solid land mass extending from the southwestern corner of what we now call California to the southeastern tip of Texas. Deep beneath Mexico's western surface, two of the earth's tectonic plates, the Pacific and American, lay tranquil. But then the geological dynamics of the earth's molten core began to change the configuration of the crust, pushing the plates apart and starting the northwesterly movement of the Pacific plate (which still continues and has created what is known as California's San Andreas Fault).

Over time, a thin sliver of Mexico stuck to that plate and was literally torn away from the mainland, separated from it by a gigantic cave-in – creating the Sea of Cortez. Lower California, commonly called Baja California, comprised its western shoreline while to the east it abutted mainland Mexico.

As the gulf widened and deepened, mountains created by the upwelling of magma from the earth's core fell into the abyss creating most of the hundred-or-so islands, irregularly scattered along both coastlines. Other islands were formed by volcanic action.

The gulf, approximately seven hundred miles long and rarely more than one hundred miles wide, was first explored in 1539 by the Spanish conquistadors of Hernando Cortez. They were sent to find Aztec treasures rumored to be in sparsely populated Baja California. While the rumors proved false, Cortez's several expeditions found rich pearl oyster beds near the tiny Indian village of La Paz, where he established the first permanent colonial settlement, proved that western Mexico was not an island, and learned that living conditions were, at best, inhospitable due to the lack of fresh water and food sources. However, Cortez's accomplishments were considered far more important in the sixteenth century than they are today. Now, his name remains

Preceding pages:
VIEWED FROM BELOW, A SCHOOL of scalloped hammerhead sharks aggregates at **El Bajo seamount.**

A TYPICAL SHORELINE IN THE southern Sea of Cortez near **La Paz.**

affixed only to some maps. For some reason, U.S. cartographers generally prefer the correct, but prosaic, appellation Gulf of California. Divers and other aficionados prefer the more romantic sounding Sea of Cortez.

Early explorers compared the Sea of Cortez to the Adriatic Sea because of its size, and to the Red Sea due to the red coloration or "red tides" caused by the periodic "bloom" of dinoflagellates. [Under favorable environmental conditions, these single-celled planktonic plants can experience explosive population increases, which in some cases cause a dangerous red tide that may result in extensive fish kills and contamination of shellfish.] While these similarities are principally accurate, the area possesses its own set of characteristics which combine to set it apart as one of the world's best diving sites.

Baja California – the Forgotten Stepchild

For over four centuries, Baja California was ignored. What it had was far outweighed by what it didn't have – mineral resources, arable land, and most importantly – fresh water. Since few forms of plant life can survive in such a harsh, arid climate, it isn't surprising that the cactus family seems to dominate the landscape. Human population has always been small and clustered around the relatively few locations that have adequate fresh water.

The sea offered sustenance to the indigenous Mexicans and exploitation to foreigners, from the earliest pirates to whalers and later commercial fishing fleets from Japan.

Even as recently as 1967, Baja California was a sleepy, agrarian backwater, visited occasionally by wealthy sport fishermen and bird hunters and a growing number of naturalists, among them Joseph Wood Krutch, who wrote: "Baja California is a wonderful example of how much bad roads can do for a country." Both the land and the Sea of Cortez were inaccessible to all but the most intrepid.

The first American invasion of Baja California occurred in 1846 when the Mexican government refused to consider a U.S. offer of $40 million for the purchase of the two Californias, Alta and Baja. What might be called a second air, land, and sea offensive began in the 1970s after the Mexican government completed three jetports, paved the 1059-mile-long Transpeninsular Highway #1, and implemented ocean-going ferry service from Baja to the mainland. Desalinization plants and deep wells provided the crucial ingredient for tourism to flourish. FoNaTur, the government corporation responsible for developing tourism, funded, planned, and started developing resort areas in and around Loreto, La Paz, and Cabo San Lucas.

While these resort areas now have over five thousand hotel rooms available for tourists, there is no sense of crowding or overbuilding. La Paz, the capital of Baja Sur (the Mexican state occupying the southern half of Baja California), has a population of approximately one hundred thousand, but it's more like a sprawling town than a city. It is also the largest and most cosmopolitan port. English is a fairly common second language. Food is basically Mexican, but Americanization has made inroads. Perhaps the best news is that Montezuma's revenge seems to have extended only to the eastern shore

SPINY RED SEA STARS ARE
among many colorful species
found in the Sea of Cortez.

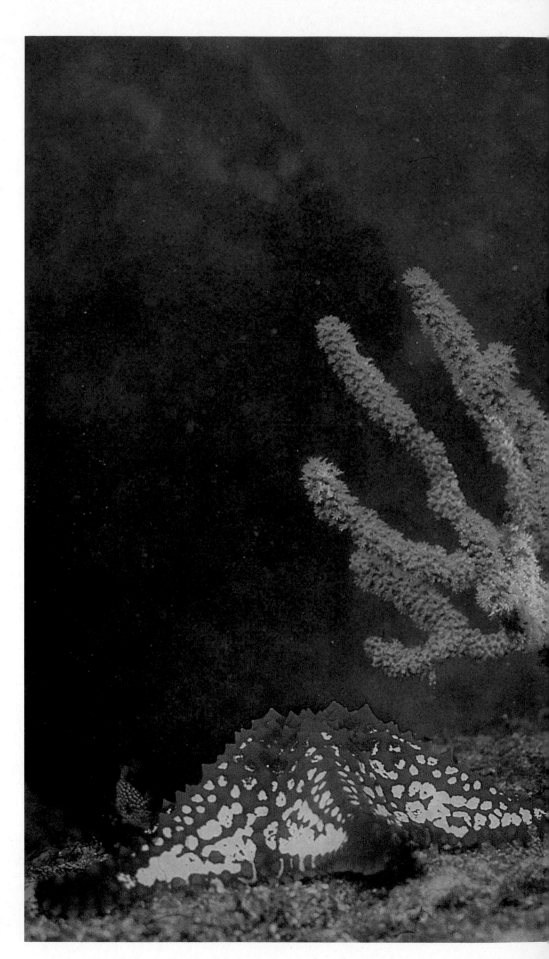

unseen from below water, launched himself into a power dive at me, intent on barking his warning to back off, but equally as careful not to hurt me. "Aye, aye, sir! Message received!" I had crossed over his invisible line of indulgence.

Like the sea lions, porpoises are not peculiar to the Sea of Cortez. Highly intelligent and clearly able to communicate, occasionally one or more will choose to interact with divers. Perhaps the most amusing fact about porpoises is their theoretical inability to attain their top speed of about twenty-three miles per hour, a theory very much akin to that which proved bumblebees can't fly. Perhaps due to their superior intelligence, porpoises have never accepted Sir James Gray's fifty-year-old calculations that related the animals' theoretical speed to its form and muscle power.

We have been entertained by schools of these delightful creatures around the world as they ventured in to ride the pressure waves created by boats' hulls. They are fun to watch but difficult to photograph underwater.

So when the *Don Jose* was cruising by Espíritu Santo island, I was surprised by my emotional reaction at seeing an oblique line of hundreds of porpoises moving in the same direction—jumping, leaping, playing like frisky colts, yet imbued with a military-drill discipline. As I contemplated the scene with a sense of awe, a finback whale breached a hundred yards off the port beam. My reverie was broken by the sound of the dinner bell.

Opposite:

A SEA LION PUP GETS AC-quainted with the camera, showing no fear.

CALIFORNIA SEA LION PUPS are fearless of divers and quite curious.

79

SLOPPY-GUTS

While resting between dives to allow excessive nitrogen bubbles to vent out of our systems, Alex Kerstitch, a marine biologist at the University of Arizona, suggested we might want to photograph a particular tube anemone, *Cerianthus*. Several were located on the eighty-foot-deep sand bottom beneath the boat, which was anchored in a cove at Isla San Francisquito. We debated whether it was worth making a dive to that depth. Given the depths and length of our earlier dives plus the time we had spent on the surface since our last dive, the dive tables allowed us a mere seventeen minutes. Alex urged us to dive. After all, John Steinbeck had described *Cerianthus* in *The Sea of Cortez* as "the sand anemone whose head is beautiful but whose body is very ugly, like rotting gray cloth." One crewman "christened Cerianthus 'sloppy guts,' and the name stuck."

But how incredibly beautiful those creatures were: fragile, delicate tentacles swaying in the slight current. Even at that depth, we could recognize the iridescent, yet subtle, colors of rose and violet. *Cerianthus* isn't rare, but it is one of the roses worth stopping to smell.

AN UNCHARTED SNAKEPIT

Only a few seamounts rise in the Sea of Cortez. The captain of *Don Jose* knew of one, a relatively well-kept secret revealed to him by a fisherman. It is nameless and appears on no charts. Ours was the only boat there. One of the seamount's small, flattened peaks was a veritable snakepit, populated by a writhing mass of panamic green moray eels (*Gymnothorax castaneus*). This isn't supposed to happen; moray eels of all species are generally solitary creatures. Occasionally a pair will be seen. They are also nocturnal, sedentary hunters who wait for their crustacean prey to wander into their range of smell.

JOHN STEINBECK CALLED THIS delicate tube anemone "sloppy guts." (Robert Boye)

AT A SEAMOUNT, ABOUT A
hundred normally nocturnal
green panamic moray eels are
found out of their holes
at midday.

81

(Morays have highly developed nasal canals with visible nostrils and holes near their eyes where the water exits.)

But there we were in broad daylight with at least one hundred eels actively moving about the pockmarked, rocky peak. Not lone eels or even pairs sliding through the crevices, but three, four, or (I photographed) five intertwined in one hole. These arm-sized undulators were defying textbook explanations of moray eel behavior, somewhat analogous to finding a flock of eagles in a communal nest. By some Darwinian anomaly, had this population adapted its behavior to suit the unique, food-laden environment of this seamount? Or was this phenomenon simply an example of the profusion of life found in the Sea of Cortez?

FUTURE STEWARDSHIP

Only posterity will know the outcome of Mexico's stewardship over the Sea of Cortez. Certainly, what we observe today is only a fraction of what was there in 1941 when John Steinbeck observed the marine life. In *The Sea of Cortez*, still difficult to get to, but if you decide to pay the price, you just might be rewarded with a magic dive.

Of all that I have enjoyed in the Sea of Cortez, five experiences stand out. Diving with whale sharks would rank as a highlight in anyone's career. At Gorda Banks off San Jose del Cabo, I was part of a crew hoping to film schooling hammerheads and whale sharks. Following the recommendations of local fishermen we chartered a ponga out to the banks, and we struck gold. The first shark I saw was at least forty feet long and weighed in the neighborhood of fifteen tons. Its mouth was at least ten feet across. Howard Hall, Lenora Carey, and I all managed to catch up with the animal and together we took an underwater tour of the banks, all three of us holding onto the animal's enormous pectoral fin. After a few minutes I let go of the pectoral and swam around to take a look at the shark. I settled on the opposite pectoral fin and rode for five or ten minutes. When I swam back to join Howard and Lenora, they were shocked to see me be-

· MICHELE HALL ENJOYS THE RARE THRILL OF RIDING A GIANT ·
manta ray.

cause they had assumed I had run low on air and been forced to surface. How large is forty feet and fifteen tons? So large that we were riding the same animal without my friends knowing I was there!

No place can be as much fun as the sea lion rookery at Los Islotes, especially in the fall when the pups demonstrate intense curiosity about divers and the cows are willing to give them free rein. In fact, at times the pups absolutely mob divers, gently mouthing their fins, snorkels, and strobes. It is all in "good fun" though and something one will never forget.

The now famous El Bajo seamount has provided me with memorable dives. In the summer of 1980, while working on a shoot for ABC's "American Sportsman," I was part of a gang that untangled a long strand of net from a large manta ray. The line had sawed a nasty cut into the manta's head and the animal was obviously relieved to have it re-

moved. For the next five days the ray remained near the seamount and we rode it at will. In fact, it often approached us. Whether it thought we were the world's largest remoras I

· THIS ADOLESCENT KING ANGELFISH HAS NOT YET ACQUIRED ·
the more regal coloration of the adult.

do not know, but it appeared as eager to have us on its back as we were to ride it and film it.

During one of my manta rides the animal swam directly into the leading edge of a school of scalloped hammerhead sharks—a hundred or more of them. As we approached the sharks I looked up and saw a marlin at the edge of the school. I tried to hold to the ray with one hand and meanwhile to take my camera and frame the manta's head in the foreground of the shot while placing the marlin and the sharks in the background. I did not get the picture I wanted because I fell off the ray while trying to compose it—but needless to say the scene is firmly entrenched in my mind.

· A PAIR OF MALE FRIGATE BIRDS COMPETE IN A MATING ·
display contest.

The mantas' ability as swimmers and their hydrodynamic design has impressed me the most. I have watched what appeared to be absolutely motionless rays easily outdistance me while I was swimming as fast as I could with a strong current at my back. They can glide much faster than I can swim, even though they do not appear to be moving at all. It is a wonderful lesson in evolution and in how remarkably well designed animals can be for their life in the marine environment.

And what is it like to dive into dense schools of scalloped hammerhead sharks? These animals commonly reach lengths of between eight and twelve feet. There have been times when I have looked overhead and seen several hundred of them. It is an astounding experience. On several occasions I found myself surrounded by sharks less than ten feet away; but I know, from first-hand experience, that I am not in danger. Nonetheless, the experience evokes some primitive emotion. The hammerheads are magnificent creatures, and somehow I can't help getting a rush out of the fact that I am seeing close at hand a natural phenomenon that only a handful of people have ever witnessed.

When I reflect on my impressions of the Cortez, I'll always remember a pinnacle dive I made near Agua Verde. Conditions were not especially good. A heavy plankton bloom near the surface made the water green and dark, but at about eighty feet down conditions improved markedly. At about 140 feet or so I discovered a basket starfish perched on a cherry red gorgonian. I remember stopping and thinking about what I was looking at and where I was. Many people can't even locate the Sea of Cortez on a map, and I was filming a creature that most don't even know exists. I wanted to just stop and look around, and at the same time I didn't have a moment to waste. It would take years to photograph the marine life in the Cortez the way I wanted to, and my bottom time was already low. At that moment I began to appreciate what a special place the Cortez is.

The land surrounding the sea is a geologist's dream. Intense volcanic activity is obvious to anyone who looks at the mountain ranges that border the water. The mountainous terrain rises sharply, providing spectacular scenery. Appreciating the natural beauty of the deserts might take more work at first. At first glance they appear barren, but people who spend a little time exploring deserts develop an intense love for them. Keen observers soon begin to appreci-

· BROWN PELICANS THRIVE IN THE FISH-LADEN WATERS ·
of the Sea of Cortez.

ate how the terrain varies, and how each stretch of desert is so vastly different from the rest. After a short time, the appeal of desert exploration is likely to capture you as it has most other visitors.

Perhaps, too, the diving in other areas of the world can equal the Cortez, but I feel confident that no place offers any better. It is the perfect spot for any diver who has a true sense of adventure. Odds are if you visit here once, the Cortez will get into your blood.

85

MICRONESIAN EMERALDS

TRUK LAGOON AND BELAU

Micronesia is a scattering of 2,141 small islands that lie like a trail of breadcrumbs sprinkled across a portion of the North Pacific Ocean the size of the United States. The total land area is less than half the size of Rhode Island. Terrain varies from flat, sandy coral islets to steep, heavily vegetated volcanic mountaintops.

Its tribal peoples, too, have always been varied. But because the islands straddled a strategic area of sea communication, international politicians lumped them together to simplify colonial governance. For over 450 years, Micronesians

MOST OF THE SUNKEN SHIPS at Truk Lagoon lie in waters surrounding three islands: from left to right are Dublon, Uman, and Fefan.

Preceding pages:
A HEAVILY ENCRUSTED MAST of the *Fujikawa Maru.*

(literally, the people of many small islands) were ruled by others. Claimed by the Spanish in 1520, the islands were left to languish in isolation until the aftermath of the Spanish-American War in 1898 when Spain sold the islands to Germany.

With the Armistice of World War I, yet another colonial government was imposed—one whose impact is still felt today. In 1919 the newly founded League of Nations granted all of Micronesia, except the United States territory of Guam, to the Japanese under a mandate not to forward "the establishment of fortifications or military and naval bases." All territory was supposed to remain open to foreigners and foreign shipping. Instead, the Japanese lowered a bamboo curtain, which culminated with their withdrawal from the League of Nations in 1935 and the annexation and arming of the islands in preparation for World War II. At the end of that war, the United Nations transferred Micronesian governance to the United States.

When they were finally given the opportunity to choose their form of political independence in the late 1970s, Micronesians opted to go four separate ways, all of which retained some form of free association with the United States. Political stability is assured, because the United States retains the responsibility to defend its former UN trusteeship. For international divers, this means convenient access to two of the world's best dive sites, Truk Lagoon and Belau. English is the language; the U.S. dollar is the currency.

Truk Lagoon, roughly forty miles in diameter, encompasses most of the

SUNSET OVER TRUK LAGOON.

islands that comprise the State of Truk, part of the recently created Federated States of Micronesia. It lies 3,600 miles west-southwest of Hawaii, seven degrees north of the Equator. Another 1,500 miles (and one more travel day) due west is the Republic of Belau, a place that used to be called Palau by its colonial governors.

Diving in these two locations is distinctly dissimilar. Truk Lagoon contains more divable shipwrecks than any other spot in the world, a historical moment encapsuled by the sea. On the other hand, the reefs of Belau, isolated by great distances from any significant land mass, comprise an almost perfect saltwater aquarium that teems with flora and fauna. Neither should be missed.

TRUK LAGOON – ANCHORAGE OF THE DEAD

Truk Lagoon was formed by a gigantic volcano that eroded into a series of asymmetrical peaks, mountaintops slowly sinking back into the three-mile depths of the surrounding Pacific Ocean. What remains are ten sizable, verdant, ruggedly hilly islands, a couple hundred islets, a huge, flat, sandy-bottomed deepwater anchorage and five deepwater passes through the 140-mile-long reef. The totality forms an incredible harbor seemingly in the middle of nowhere. The circular, surrounding reef is topped by a necklace of platinum surf and sand strung randomly with small, irregularly shaped emeralds of lush vegetation and storybook beaches. Truly, this is one of the most beautiful of all atolls. The reef protects the lagoon, its people, and the artifacts displayed in the world's largest underwater museum, what some call the "Ghost Fleet" of the Japanese Imperial Navy.

The World's Largest Underwater Museum

Nowhere else in the world can divers experience the awesome beauty created by the detritus of war. And nowhere else exists a museum whose curators have not fully cataloged its contents. While most of the known wrecks are concentrated in the fleet anchorages around the islands of Dublon, Fefan, and Uman, others are distributed throughout the lagoon. New wrecks are still being discovered. The forty-three-year solitude of the destroyer *Fumitsuki* was broken only in April 1987, providing access to one of the few sunken ships of war.

A Three-Ring Circus

Nothing can prepare uninitiated divers for the thrill and excitement of Truk Lagoon's three main attractions, the wrecks of the *Shinkoko Maru*, *Sankisan Maru*, and *Fujikawa Maru*. They are world-class acts without parallel, bedecked with all the glitter, glitz, and glow of a laser color show. Magically, these ships have transformed into complete coral reefs. Hard corals, soft

THE DEEP RED COLOR OF this tunicate colony on the hull of the *Fujikawa Maru* is very unusual.

FLOWERLIKE TUBASTREA
coral polyps flourish on the hull
of the *Shinkoku Maru*.

corals, invertebrates, crustaceans, and exotic reef fishes compete for a moment's exposure to your eye; large animals — sharks, rays, ocean spade fish, and schools of jacks — circle the arena. From the anemones that grow over the decks, hulls and surfaces, anemonefishes of several varieties dart in and out of their multihued hosts. Even the underwater Emmet Kelly, the clown trigger fish, dashes into the center ring.

Looming above this arena are the ghostly baker towers and masts supporting the wires and cables of the aerial acts: colorful whip corals hang from above with crinoids of every color and design, waving to viewers. A large lionfish ventures out from beneath the stern gun of the *Fujikawa* for an afternoon performance. Can this experience be a hallucination, a mirage?

The panoply of the show distracts from the funereal actuality, but can't hide it. Clearly the superstructures of this circus of life are machines of war. A circular plume worm growing on the detonator of a 120mm naval shell disguises it, but it is still a deadly weapon. The stark function of a Zero fighter plane can't be hidden; it is still a killing machine. A machine gun, encrusted with coral and sponge, is almost nondescript, but the hundreds of bullets lying in the gun tub beneath give mute testimony to its former mission.

Only the human remains have been removed from these once macabre wrecks. At the behest of the Japanese government, divers recovered the bones of the dead in the early 1980s. They were cremated at the site of a Shinto shrine, a final resting place of dignity.

duce convulsions at depths greater than 140 feet) are all real possibilities, especially on a wreck like the *San Francisco Maru* where three military tanks sit on the deck at 165 feet. One way the guides maintain their enviable safety record is by minimizing risk.

Photographic opportunities abound, from the large propeller of the *Gosei Maru* to the twin propellers of *Rio De Janeiro Maru*, its dimpled and punctured forward plates caused by the interior explosions of its cargo of ammunition. The *Yamagiri Maru's* No. 3 hold contains one of the oddities of World War II, a jumble of man-sized projectiles. Eighteen inches in diameter and each weighing a ton and a half, they were the largest naval ordnance ever built and were destined to replenish the magazines of the super battleship *Musashi.*

A Mystery of Marine Biology

The four-hundred-fifty-foot *Kiyozumi Maru* is an ugly wreck, wrapped in a coating of algae, almost devoid of coral and other animal life. It best exemplifies the disparities of marine life found on the wrecks. Why are some so gaudily adorned while others lie almost naked? Various hypotheses have

Opposite:

HARD AND SOFT CORALS compete for space on the deck of the *Fujikawa Maru.*

IN THE WHEELHOUSE OF THE *Shinkoku Maru,* **the engine telegraph stands idle.**

been offered by marine biologists: differences in the effectiveness of antifouling paint, which has retarded growth of marine organisms; the leaching out of various toxic chemicals from munitions or fuels, preventing most life forms; and the theory that each wreck has its own unique electrical field that either inhibits or promotes growth of marine life. Further complicating the mystery is the finding that many species found on the *Shinkoku, Fujikawa,* and *Sanki-san* grow at a faster rate there than they do under similar conditions on a coral reef. In addition, these three wrecks lie in widely different locations and are interspersed with dozens of less beautiful ones.

Getting There

Air Micronesia enjoys monopoly status as the sole air carrier flying scheduled local service into Micronesia. Because the 3,600-mile trip westward from Hawaii takes over ten hours, departures are scheduled for early morning. Thus, a one-night layover is required. But Air Mike's schedules are sometimes fluid and difficult to verify. Passengers should not rely on tickets marked "confirmed." Wary divers should confirm their next morning's flight at the airport. And *definitely* reconfirm return reservations at least seventy-two hours in advance. Failure to do so can lose you a seat!

Truk at Ebb Tide
Above water, Truk is a naturally beautiful place, but it isn't pretty. In fact, it is downright depressing. Like New York City, Truk looks best from the air — for closer inspection reveals an unkempt shabbiness. Sprinkled among the verdant growth are growing patches of rust — abandoned cars, trucks, boats, refrigerators, and television sets that litter these tiny islands. Soda and beer cans, bottles, and multihued plastics of all sizes seem to grow like the perennial wildflowers — everywhere.

Walking around the capital town of Moen on the main island of the

CASES OF SMALL-CALIBER RI-
fle and machine gun ammunition
are scattered around the holds of
the *Sankisan Maru.*

returned. When four high-rise hotels are completed, Belau will become another honeymoon destination for young Japanese. Belau isn't the sort of place where Americans drop in for a few days of diving. But for Japanese, the trip is the equivalent of a flight from New York to the Virgin Islands.

Getting There

For many years, dive tour operators have offered package deals that link diving in Belau and Truk Lagoon. Although such tours seem costly and time-consuming, in the long run they are worth it, because the expense of including Belau in your itinerary is minimal. By the time you get as far as Truk, most of the airfare cost is behind you. But the allure of Belau is only fifteen hundred air miles and another night away.

Belau's economy depends upon tourists. They are catered to at first-class hotels and by topnotch dive operators who rely on their yen and dollars. Dive boats are generally fast, open skiffs designed to cover large expanses of water quickly. They offer little, if any, protection from the sun and virtually no comfort when pounding over wavelets at high speed. However, some of the best sites are twenty to twenty-five miles from the dock. Thus, to get there and back, you sacrifice your body. For some, the saving grace is knowing that a cold beer will always be waiting upon their return. While it may be a tiny country with a faltering economy, beer is its second largest import.

The Paradox of Accessibility

The alternative to spending hours each day skittering across the lagoon is to opt for a live-aboard boat. Some of the best sites in Belau are simply out of range for land-based divers. The only way to see some of the exciting passes and barrier walls is from a floating hotel. The paradox, however, lies in the logistical difficulty of getting the customers to the merchandise. Diving in Belau is a cottage industry. Currently, there is only one live-aboard boat. While it enjoys an excellent reputation, it carries only six passengers.

People with a Purpose

Belauans are obviously different than the peoples of other Micronesian island groups. Historically, they were the most warlike of all the tribes. Furthermore, due to their isolated location at the southwestern extremity, their bloodlines were intermixed with Malay, Melanesian, and, to a great extent, Japanese and English.

Belauans are handsome, alert, and industrious. They seem to have done more with their fair share of post-colonial largess. Houses are neat and painted; litter seems to find its way to the dump; schoolyards are filled with neatly uniformed children. While Belauans, like the Trukese, have major economic problems, they are confronting them with a sense of purpose. Their get-up-and-go attitude is based on cultural mores that favor competition. Prestige equates with wealth. Belauans exhibit a sense of industry not found elsewhere in Micronesia.

Nothing illustrates this better than the pioneering work being done at

Opposite:
SOME SEA FANS ARE LARGE enough to cover a banquet table.

the Micronesian Mariculture Demonstration Center in Koror. Belauan marine biologists have perfected breeding techniques to reproduce commercial quantities of what was once a staple food throughout the Pacific Basin, the giant clam.

Brobdingnagian Clams

Probably the largest invertebrates ever known are a family of bivalve molluscs commonly called giant clams. Yet one species in particular, *Tridacna gigas*, is rarely found in its mature, giant state anymore, because their adductor muscles have long since been cut out for an Asian feast. Demand for the adductor muscle is huge in the Orient. Markets in Taiwan, Japan, Hong Kong, and Singapore will pay up to seventy dollars per pound for this delicacy.

Thus, we were excited to find seven or eight live shells in chest-high water off one of the Rock Islands. The clams ranged from four to five feet long, weighing perhaps a half-ton each. Fist-sized siphons were surrounded by fleshy mantles of emerald green or indigo blue, embroidered with psychedelic patterns of contrasting and complementary colors.

Gingerly touching a mantle, we watched the mammoth shell slowly close its gates in a grip that was long believed to be able to capture a hapless diver's foot. But the man-eater image proved to be a myth. Our experiment revealed that for a human to be caught by a giant tridacna, he would have to have a foot of superhuman proportions. Quite simply, the mantles are so fleshy that the shells can't close enough either to capture a victim — or to protect themselves from the sharp knives of Taiwanese or Japanese pirates.

The economic incentive for poaching is enormous throughout the Pa-

SCIENTISTS HAVE SPECULATED that the cobalt sea star's blue coloration serves as a sunscreen. (Robert Boye)

cific; however, the impetus to replenish vanishing stocks of this staple food, but endangered species, is even greater. If they survive their first week of larval life, these clams develop one of the most efficient food sources in nature. Their mantles are host to symbiotic unicell algae, zooxanthillae, that use sunlight to produce organic compounds that, in turn, are used as food by the clams. While they also derive some nutriment from filtered plankton, the clams appear to rely mostly on the zooxanthellae for food. Thus, if left to their own devices, these autotrophic, or "self-feeding," giants grow to marketable size in three years. No one knows how long it takes tridacna to attain the size we saw, but it only takes seconds to kill one.

Alabaster Banquet Tables
In the unblemished coral gardens of Belau grow some of the world's largest and most delicate table corals, species of the Acroporidae family. Almost-wafer-thin discs, fifteen or more feet in diameter, are balanced on slender pedestals, like banquet tables designed by Alvar Aalto, the Finnish architect.

Closer examination reveals a host of tiny groupies, banded humbugs (*Dascyllus aruanus*), who live as a colony within the well-defined perimeter. Plankton feeders, they live in the tiny niches afforded by the fragile coral. Popping up into the current, they are served a dinner of nutrient-rich water. At the first sign of danger, the fish all drop as one into the coral's intricate web, like crumbs caught in cracks.

The Right Place
At the southwestern extreme of the Belauan lagoon lies Ngemelis Island, a quarter-mile boomerang shape of greenery and sand sitting atop a spectacular undersea wall. The island's location protects it from the prevailing northeasterly winds that blow from April through November. Even when the south-westerlies blow during the rest of the year, the eastern edge of the eight-hundred-foot-deep wall is in the lee. Ngemelis is one side of a mile-wide funnel through which the six-foot tides pour nourishment into the lagoon. At the right time, practically anything may be seen here; it is the right place.

Waiting for the incoming tide, we anchored the skiff on the flats, which were still awash at low tide. As we waded through the coral toward the beach, we were fascinated by the hordes of tiny reef fishes protected by the mazes of delicate hard corals. Color was almost totally absent, until we were struck by the brilliant blue of the cobalt sea star (*Linckia laevigata*). Most sea stars prowl at night, but the cobalt's habitat is where we were – daylight in shallow flats. Scientists have speculated that the animal's blue coloration is a sun-screen. Whatever the reason, the effect is strikingly beautiful.

Gliding down the wall with the tide's change, we could pick our depth to assay the vast array of soft corals opening in the tidal flow. Gorgonians and siphonogorgias competed for space with sea-fan tablecloths large enough to cover the acropora banquet tables. Brilliantly colored tree corals grow to three-foot heights. Colors are deceiving, because some species fluoresce, emitting colors visible to the eye but not to film.

Some species of fish, groupers and sharks for example, almost never school. Thus, when four of us turned our backs to the wall, we were flabbergasted when a school of grey reef sharks slid along the edge of the dropoff. Like the Navy's famed precision flying team the Blue Angels, the eight animals maintained their perfect geometric pattern until they were lost in the indigo haze.

But why did these powerful plunderers school? Certainly, the reason wasn't mutual protection, because sharks have few natural predators. We hypothesized their formation was an example of cooperative hunting, something akin to the U-boat wolfpacks of World War II.

Maybe, just maybe, at this pass you might see one of the solitary angelfish that are rare in the world but occasionally seen in Belau. The yellow-faced angelfish (*Euxiphipops xanthometapon*) is unmistakable, with its intricately blue-scrawled surgical mask below its bright yellow-orange eye mask.

How Long? Uolong!

One afternoon our dive guide announced the tide was right for a drift dive in the Uolong Channel, just beyond the Rock Islands. The channel itself was a mile-long, sand-bottomed straightaway, six lanes wide with a median strip of coral, ending in a coral-walled cul-de-sac. Drift was an exaggeration; drag race was closer to reality – for the faster the current flows, the more difficult it becomes to stop or to hold onto the reef. Our cameras were useless. Stopping on the world's largest underwater waterslide to focus a camera was almost impossible. It was shallow, narrow, and fast. So we played like little kids, somersaulting – forwards and backwards – until the water jet turned off where the boat was waiting. How long did it take? Uolong!

A Jellyfish Bath

The limestone erosion that shaped Belau's unique topography also created one of its oddities, two-dozen inland marine lakes. All are connected by tunnels, at or below sea level, to tidal salt water. Thus, lake water levels are the same as the surrounding coves. Depending upon the length and complexity of the tunnels, some lakes are more brackish than others. Each seems to be a showcase for one predominant species.

By climbing, crawling, snorkeling, and swimming, divers can negotiate the entrance to Jellyfish Marine Lake on Koror. Its algae-encrusted shore isn't inviting, but small communities of flame ascidians (*Polycarpa simplex*) make perimeter reconnaissance worthwhile. Once in the tepid water, divers are surrounded by tens of thousands of dwarfed jellyfish (*Mastigias papua*). Darwin would revel in his theories proven true. For here, with a distinctly different environment, these animals have shrunken into miniature form. Furthermore, their stinging tentacles have shriveled into useless, unneeded weapons.

Ominous Rumors

Few, if any, sites in the world are as complete and compact as Belau. From the

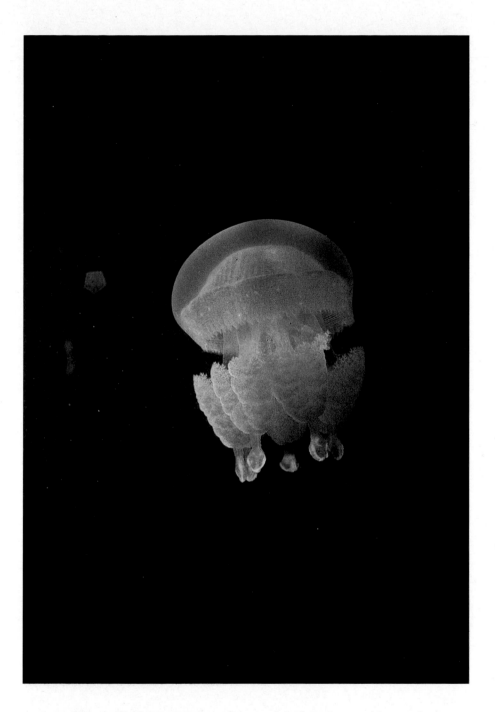

109

near perfect atoll of Kayangel to the wrecks of Japanese ships and planes, divers have a myriad of readily accessible opportunities: blue holes, caves, caverns, drop-offs, passes, walls. Its marine flora and fauna rival the best in the world. This is a place meant to be seen, admired, and protected.

But all of this is a poker chip in the bargaining and bluffing game between the governments of the Philippines and the United States. Leases on the U.S. air and naval bases expire in a few years. As demands for more foreign aid and higher rents have increased, U.S. diplomats have made it clear that these military facilities can be transferred to Belau. Divers should hope the two governments reach a long-term accord to keep the bases in the Philippines. Moving even a fraction of the naval facilities to the Belauan lagoon could have a devastating impact on the Tiffany of the Sea.

MICRONESIA

O f the more than two thousand islands that comprise the sprawling Pacific region called Micronesia, two atolls stand out as the most amazing undersea environments in the world today—not only unique to this area but to the entire Pacific Ocean. They are the places I love best.

T R U K   L A G O O N

This is one of the world's most extraordinary diving locations. Truk Lagoon is an underwater time capsule in which events and objects have been frozen since the close of World War II. Veteran travelers have described it as one of the Seven Underwater Wonders of the World. This vast coral lagoon measuring 38 miles in diameter and reaching depths of 240 feet was Japan's version of Pearl Harbor, once the headquarters of the Combined Japanese Imperial Navy.

Like Pearl Harbor, Truk Lagoon fell victim to a sudden and violent carrier attack. During the course of two days and one night Allied Forces rained a continuous hailstone of bombs, bullets, and torpedoes that eventually sank fifty Japanese ships and hundreds of aircraft. Today, these steely monuments stand as a silent memorial to a great and tragic war, a watery grave that remains virtually intact and contains a treasure house of wartime artifacts.

Yet, the lagoon is much more than a wreck diver's paradise. Its warm tropical waters have transformed these maritime hulks into fantastic artificial reefs. Truk's most notable wrecks are draped in a living tapestry of stony coral formations, brightly colored soft corals, sponges, anenomes, oysters, and a thousand other delicate marine organisms. They are a wonderland for the underwater photographer.

There is a mystery about this remarkable transformation. What is it about these ships that has made them more beautiful than any in the Pacific? Why do certain wrecks in Truk Lagoon appear as ornate as Christmas trees while others nearby remain in a dusty tomb? While these questions remain unanswered, the sites themselves provoke thought and wonderment. Wrecks such as the *Fujikawa Maru*, *Sankisan Maru*, and *Shinkoku Maru* are carpeted with a veritable jungle of marine life. The soft corals are so thick that they obscure the outline of the ships' decks, guns, and superstructure. These great wrecks host more marine life than many coral reefs.

And because of this, they serve as a beacon for fish. Tucked in the folds of these vibrant environments are clownfish, lionfish, pipefish, and scores of other exotic species. Great clouds of baitfish move across the watery decks like a swarm of locusts. And circling the wrecks' perimeters

· MUSHROOM-SHAPED ALGAE CLUSTER ON THE HULL ·
of the *Shinkoku Maru*. (Paul Tzimoulis)

V I G N E T T E   B Y   G E R I   M U R P H Y

are the pelagic predators—jacks, tuna, mackerel, and an occasional shark.

This miracle of life is Truk Lagoon's most compelling attraction. I have returned there frequently simply to wit-

· A DIVER INSPECTS A HATCH ·
on the Japanese submarine
I–169, which lies in 125 feet of
water. (Paul Tzimoulis)

ness and photograph the transformation of these incredible wrecks into the most beautiful artificial reefs I have ever seen.

PALAU LAGOON (BELAU)

Belau is the anithesis of its Micronesian partner. While Truk offers a sharply delineated focus on a single phenomenon, the undersea sights and experiences of Belau are so diverse that it can be mind-boggling for the first-time visitor.

While Truk Lagoon is circular in shape and occupied by a few large islands, Belau Lagoon is long and slender, populated by hundreds of tiny rock islets, as well as some major ones. This lagoon is much larger, measuring some ninety miles across. But what makes Belau so remarkable is its remarkable inventory of marine life—a cornucopia of exotic and rare ocean creatures that challenge the skills of even the most seasoned underwater photographer. It would take a diver a lifetime to photograph everything Belau has to offer.

It is best known to divers for its spectacular drop-offs. Many of these vertical coral walls begin just under the surface and plummet vertically to depths of nine hundred feet or more. Wall sites such as Ngemelis, Peleliu, Siaes Tunnel, and Blue Holes, are legendary among underwater photog-

raphers. This is truly high-voltage diving—you are greeted by a kaleidoscope of colorful soft corals, gigantic fans, and a rush of fish action. Encounters with schools of barracuda, giant tuna, manta rays, and sharks are the norm. The diver must keep one hand on the camera shutter every moment, poised for one action shot after another.

And while Belau's drop-offs are indeed outstanding, there is far more to see. This vast coral lagoon is dotted with hundreds of tiny coral islands, each one topped with an emerald green covering of jungle—wild, uninhabited, and for the most part undisturbed. These are a leftover from a primeval era. Tiny marine organisms along the water's edge have burrowed into the limestone, chiseling each formation into a mushroom-shaped profile. While the surrounding waters are not as clear as in the outer drop-offs, they are filled with a marvelous array of delicate and beautiful creatures.

A spot called the Arch is an underwater channel between two islands, carpeted with hundreds of small soft corals. Each one is a different color, a different shade. And among these islands you will often find the giant tridacna clams, some weighing up to six hundred pounds. Many kinds of small crabs and shrimp thrive here, providing an endless supply of photographic subjects.

If diving around the outer edges of the rock islands were not enough, an even more striking experience awaits the more adventuresome. Trapped within some of the large islands are saltwater lakes that have been separated from the rest of the lagoon for thousands of years. Contained here are rare subspecies of marine life that have adapted and evolved over the eons. Jellyfish Lake, for example, contains a colony of thousands of jellyfish that have lost their ability to sting with their tentacles. Food supply is plentiful and predators nonexistent, so the jellyfish had no need for their defensive mechanisms.

Another feature of Belau's rock islands can provide a journey into fantasyland: Beneath several of the islands are underwater caves and caverns that can dazzle the senses. Chandelier Cave near Koror is a series of five separate chambers connected by tunnels. Hanging from the ceilings are stalactites in sparkling shades of white, pearl and crystal. These are considered some of the most beautiful underwater caves in the world.

Most of Belau is still a wilderness, unpopulated and untamed. It is one of those very special places where the photographer can come close to nature and yet not destroy it. It is my dream to return again and again to this magical spot before it is gone forever.

GEMS
OF THE
CARIBBEAN

When the seeds of coral reef life were cast on the world's tropical oceans and seas, distribution was uneven. Some waters received species by the thousands, others by the hundreds. Most got a mere smattering. The Caribbean Sea, a part of the Atlantic Ocean bounded by Central America, the West Indies, and South America, is one of the areas blessed with an abundance of marine species. In fact, it is the only part of the Atlantic Ocean that enjoys such diversity.

Captured within the sweep of the three land areas that comprise the West Indies (the

116

SNORKLERS ENJOY THE CLEAR
waters of the Caribbean.

PORKFISH (FOREGROUND) CO-
habit a reef crevice with their
cousins, the blue striped grunts.

of the Netherlands Antilles, a Dutch colony, and the Bahamas is an independent country. They are all extremely stable politically and totally unthreatening to tourists. Divers are welcome and treated as guests.

For Americans, perhaps the best news about the Caribbean basin is the cost. To a large extent, market forces make diving there one of the best bargains in the world. It is a sizable and lucrative market for airlines and dive operators. Consequently, the combination of competition, limited air miles, and the relatively stable buying power of the dollar place Caribbean diving within the grasp of hundreds of thousands of North Americans. In addition, to keep costs low and turnover high, dive operators tend to offer package deals based on one-week trips.

THE WEATHER – WHETHER OR NOT?

Winter weather conditions (mid-December through March) can affect diving conditions just as much in the Caribbean as they do elsewhere in the Northern Hemisphere. While it doesn't snow, it can blow – long and hard. High seas can destroy visibility and severely limit dive site options. On the other hand, we have enjoyed summer-like calms in mid-January with incredible visibility. It's a matter of choice and chance, but the weather odds are stacked against you during the winter months. However, they improve as you go further south. Bonaire, located just sixty miles off the coast of Venezuela, enjoys a bountiful supply of excellent weather year-round.

RUM CAY – THE BAHAMAS' BEST-KEPT SECRET

The islands of the Bahamas and Turks and Caicos are strung on a line off the coast of south Florida and extend for almost six hundred miles to the southeast. They form a levee of limestone plateaus between the southern Atlantic and the Caribbean Sea. Like the Belauan archipelago, the islands sit atop a range of submerged mountains, some over five miles high.

Of the twelve or fifteen major islands in the Bahamas that offer diving opportunities, we prefer one of the most southerly and least developed, Rum Cay. We consider it a jewel, perhaps because it reminds us of the unspoiled island where we spent our honeymoon thirty years ago, that place where we first viewed the underwater world. Unlike many Caribbean islands, Rum Cay still has beaches that few walk and pristine reefs that fewer see. A plane flight from Fort Lauderdale takes less than three hours and is guaranteed to have no more than ten passengers. Only small aircraft can land on the island's 2,400-foot crushed-coral runway. Crowds aren't found on Rum Cay. In fact, the permanent population of the thirty-square-mile island is less than eighty.

No telephones ring and no televisions blare. There aren't any. This is a place for rest, reading, and relaxation when you aren't out diving on the dazzling, unspoiled reefs. Although the location is remote, the living accom-

WHEN PROVOKED, THE FOUR-inch-long sharpnose puffer inflates itself with water.

119

ELKHORN CORAL IS USUALLY
found in shallow water.

modations, the food, and the diving facilities are all first-class.

The Rum Cay Club is the island's only hotel and its major employer. Sitting on a low southern bluff, the club overlooks several dive sites and the daily sunsets. Its dive shop was overbuilt, equipped to service fifty divers, while the club's capacity is twenty-four. Its photo lab rivals the best we've seen. Divers here are a captive audience, but we can't imagine any other spot in the Bahamas where we would rather be prisoners.

Fishing is only for local subsistence and there is practically no population. Thus, the reefs are still a balanced marine community with a goodly number of site-attached fishes still present. Reef walls are more like slopes than sheer faces. Some are pocked with limestone caves that afford protected resting places for sea turtles and trees of black coral.

Bushy black coral (*Antipathes salix*) is probably the most commonly observed form of antipatharian found in this part of the world. Generally, this species appears in shades of brown, gray, or green, the pigmentation of its polyps. So I was intrigued when the divemaster offered to show me a giant albino tree growing inside the mouth of a cave. It was stark white and amazing to behold.

ROBERT FROST'S UNDERSEA WOODS

On a scallop of flat, sandy bottom less than one hundred yards off Rum Cay's shore stands a nursery of filter-feeding sea feathers (*Pseudopterogorgia sp.*), sea whips (*Gorgonacea*), and sea rods (*Muricea sp.*). There they thrive and grow to gigantic size. Divers are dwarfed and humbled by twelve-foot canopies of colonial polyps. The scene is reminiscent of a Robert Frost poem. A forest of weeping birch, willow, and aspen, branches laden with an icing of wet snow, sways in the breeze of ocean surge.

QUICK ON THE TRIGGER

Farther down the south shore once, beneath a shoal of horse-eye jacks (*Caranx latus*) patrolling their private grotto at eighty feet, my eye caught an unfamiliar pattern that swam with the awkward wobble of a triggerfish. Then, as I split the jacks' formation to get closer, a trigger popped up in alarm above me, its blue body speckled with trails of black dots. Before I could get within camera range, the sargassum triggerfish (*Xanthichthys ringens*) had darted into a crack in the limestone. While the species isn't rare, it is rarely seen, because it normally lives its solitary life in depths greater than one hundred feet.

Moments later, a giant green turtle swam by us. Once a common sight throughout the world's warm waters, they are now an endangered species, an example of man's predation. Unspoiled islands and surrounding reefs used to be common, too. Now islands like Rum Cay are fewer and farther between.

BELIZE – A HAVEN FOR NATURALISTS

A thousand miles west-southwest of Rum Cay, tucked under the bulge of Mexico's Yucatán Peninsula, lies Belize. Until 1981 when its 150,000 citizens gained independence, it was called British Honduras. Strangely enough, this Massachusetts-sized country shares borders with Mexico to the north and Guatemala on the west and south, not Honduras. Its eastern border faces the Caribbean Sea and is marked by the longest barrier reef in the Western Hemisphere. Hundreds of sand cays lie on or inside the reef, surrounded by silty water from the numerous fresh-water rivers. Due to the suffocating effects of silt, hard corals do not flourish along much of the reef. Outside the reef, however, the water turns from muddy brown to familiar shades of blue. There, beyond the barrier, is where divers will find the best of Belize; three

SCHOOLS OF HORSE-EYE JACKS
prowl most Caribbean reefs.

atolls – Turneffe Islands, Glovers Reef, and Lighthouse Reef.

From the rugged Maya Mountains to the low swamplands, the country is green. Blessed by abundant rainfall and sun, the land supports an agricultural economy based mainly on sugar cane, cattle, citrus fruits, and cocoa. The sea supplies export quantities of lobster and conch. But Belize is a poor country and unemployment is high. Many pre-Columbian sites dot the countryside, some within easy driving distance of Belize City, the country's coastal entry point. Farther away are wildlife refuges where the endangered cats may be seen: jaguar, puma, ocelot, margay, and jaguarundi. Tourism offers a variety of opportunities in addition to diving.

GETTING THERE

At last count, four scheduled airlines (including two U.S. carriers) fly into Belize City from Houston, New Orleans, and Miami. Getting there is easy. Two or three hours separate North Americans from Central America's culture. As the plane taxis to the terminal, it passes camouflaged, sandbagged revetments containing British Harrier jump-jets, mute evidence of Great Britain's

DIVERS RARELY SEE TUR-
tles mating.

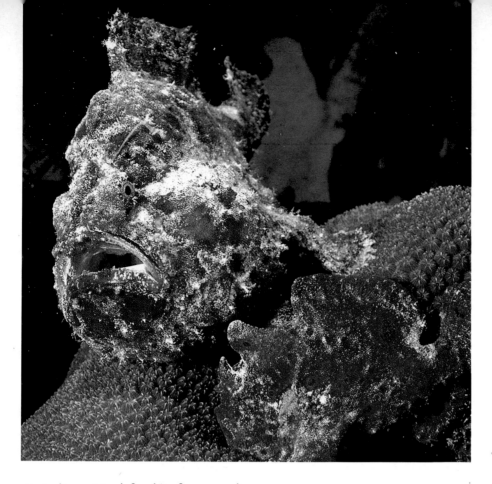

commitment to defend its former colony.

The former capital city of 50,000 is built around the mouth of Haulover Creek on what used to be a swamp, barely above sea level. Belize City was so badly damaged by a hurricane in 1961 that the government was moved fifty miles inland to the city of Belmopan. Today, it is an interesting architectural blend of Victorian gingerbread, mostly gone to rot, and new concrete buildings. Decay is winning. Open drainage canals seem to function as sewers. Floating garbage congregates in the creek behind the main market. But in spite of urban blight, there are some good hotels and decent restaurants. However, visitors are warned against nighttime strolls.

During business hours, it's quite safe to walk off the main streets to the woodcarvers' shops, a jaunt well worth the minimal effort. These families of skillful carvers fashion exquisite reproductions of fishes, turtles, porpoises, and manta rays out of exotic hardwoods. Curiously, we had seen an identical art form in a Polynesian village on the island of Pohnpei, ten thousand miles to the west.

LIGHTHOUSE REEF

Each of the three atolls outside the reef is worthy of a separate trip. All are reached from Belize City. But Lighthouse Reef best typifies what is there to be seen. As an added delight, it offers the opportunity to dive in what may be the world's largest blue hole. ["Blue holes," vertical caverns, are found on many reefs. They are generally thought to have formed when cave systems that developed in the reefs during periods of low sea level have collapsed.] Also, nearby, lies Half Moon Cay with its picturesque lighthouse and colony of almost extinct red-footed booby birds. Since Lighthouse Reef is seventy miles

to preserve and protect the reefs. By 1971, he had convinced the government to outlaw spearfishing in Bonaire. Recognizing that anchor damage to the reefs was accelerating their degradation, he initiated the installation of permanent anchorage buoys at dive sites. (Marine ecologists have estimated that each time an anchor and anchorchain is dropped on a coral reef, serious damage is inflicted on one square yard of reef surface.)

In 1975 when prominent dive operator Peter Hughes arrived to start a competitive business, Don agreed to let Peter's boats use his buoys on the condition that Peter install another six buoys at his own expense, which they would both use. Don's parade gained more and more followers, including key government officials. All believed that by protecting, preserving, and managing the reefs, they could both bolster and sustain the economy. Healthy reefs meant healthy business, more tourists, and more jobs.

Finally, in 1979 the Netherlands Antilles National Parks Foundation received a grant from the World Wildlife Fund to create a marine park in Bonaire. The object was to preserve and protect *all* reefs as well as the seagrasses and mangrove swamps of the lagoon Lac. By legal definition, the Bonaire Marine Park extends from "the seabottom and the overlying waters from the highwater tidemark down to the 60m (200 ft.) depth contour." To manage and control the park, legislation called for ongoing research and control. Together with law enforcement and education, this has led to rules and regulations that seem to benefit all. The proof is in the diving!

Bonaire's Marine Park is like an aquarium with forty-four separate tanks (dive sites) grouped into six categories according to reef characteristics. Except that this aquarium has no walls. Visitors freely mingle with the myriad of animals, from tiny nudibranchs to curious moray eels. In a typical one-week vacation, it would be difficult to dive even half the available sites. Perhaps that's why so many divers return to Bonaire, a theme park for everyone.

didn't expect to see anything much when snorkeling over the sandy bottom. But within minutes, we had found queen and helmet conch in the eel grass, several tiny octopuses with shells piled outside their lairs, a Caribbean stingray (*Himantura schmardae*) grovelling in the sand, a small, spotted moray (*Gymnothorax moringa*), a patch of garden eels (*Nystactichtys halis*), schools of squid and halfbeaks, and a lonesome, lined seahorse (*Hippocampus erectus*) clinging to a strand of grass. I was flabbergasted to see these animals living within fifty yards of a sixty-room hotel. Clearly, management takes ecology seriously.

Bloody Bay Wall

Both Cayman Brac and Little Cayman are narrow islands that lie on an east-west axis. Consequently, when winter winds howl out of the northeast making diving impossible due to choppy waves and strong currents, dive sites are always available on the leeward side. However, Little Cayman's famed Bloody Bay Wall is exposed to northerly winds and may, at times, be just as inaccessible as Grand Cayman's North Wall.

The late Philippe Cousteau called this one of the best diving sites he had ever seen, maybe even the best. I concur. This wall is exquisite, a microcosm

of virtually every life form, densely packed onto its face or swimming nearby. Unlike Cayman's North Wall, Bloody Bay Wall starts in fairly shallow water, fifteen to twenty feet. This gives divers the advantage of not having to make deep dives in order to see a lot. However, with so much to see, it is impossible to see it all.

For example, if anyone could exercise the self-discipline to limit observation solely to sponges, over thirty varieties can be found here. Their color and form are kaleidoscopic, ranging from tiny white cryptic sponges (*Leucandra aspera*) to bright yellow calcareous (*Leucosolenia canariensis*) and orange elephant ear (*Agelas clathrodes*). Azure vase sponges (*Callyspongia plicifera*) may nestle next to pink vases (*Dasychalina cyathina*) with green finger sponges (*Iotrochota birotulata*) in the background.

But even if a diver focused on sponges alone, he would see the other animals that live commensally or parasitically among them. The large, reddish-brown irritating sponge (*Neofibularia nolitangere*) is not eye-catching. Only its nickname, dread red, betrays the pain that can be inflicted by even casual contact. However, under artificial light, its true scarlet red color is revealed, as well as hundreds of parasitic sponge worms (*Syllis spongicola*). Any of several species of shrimp or brittle stars may be residents, as well.

Turks and Caicos government was considered stable until 1985 when the chief minister, one of four cabinet ministers, and one of eleven elected legislators were arrested in Miami for conspiring to set up a cocaine-smuggling operation. They were convicted and sentenced to prison. The British governor general suspended self-government for three years. Other than this attempt at big league crime, petty larceny is about as serious as it gets on the islands. Tourists are safe.

Underwater Aria

Enveloped in the sound of our own mechanical respiration a background of gray noises, our concentration was visual. Cameras record images, not sounds. Thus, I don't know how long we listened to an alien noise before it registered to stop looking and start listening. What I first thought was a malfunctioning regulator had a haunting, wistful melody. Finally, concentrating on the tune, I realized that it didn't seem to repeat itself like the music composed by humans. Slowly the realization dawned on me. The failure of the melody to repeat was the hallmark of a humpback whale's ethereal song. We were eavesdropping on one or more of the hundreds that normally migrate through these waters twice a year.

At dusk a few days before, the *Sea Dancer* had mingled with a pod of

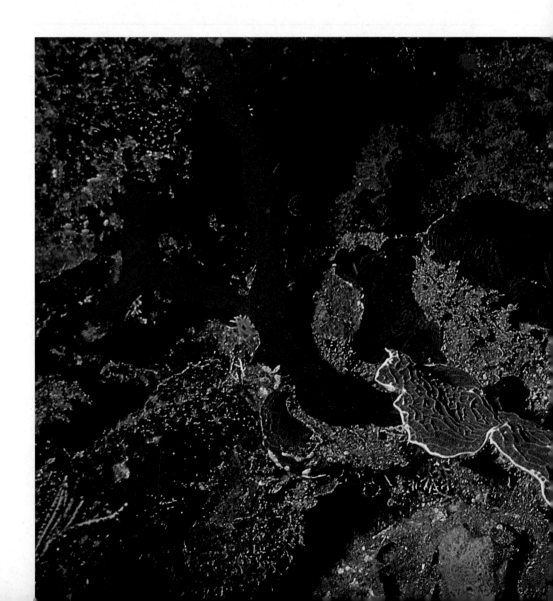

these leviathans, two cows supporting a calf under the watchful eye of a bull. With no apparent course in their migratory path, they meandered off the shore of Grand Turk. As light failed, we broke off our escort and returned to a shallower anchorage. Hours later, around midnight, two women were talking on the forward deck when their moonlit reverie was broken by the unmistakable noise and smell of a breaching whale — fifty feet off the bow and heading astern. They ran to the dive platform just as the surface split. Twenty feet off, they witnessed a forty-ton prowler that left no footprints.

An Inflatable Shark

We were returning from an unsuccessful underwater search for the eagle rays we had seen earlier on South Caicos's wall. Video wizard Stu Cummings frantically waved us toward an open-ended grotto. Nestled up against the coral wall on the wide, sandy bottom was a stationary seven-foot bull shark (*Carcharhinus leucas*). I slipped down onto the sand beside it, about five feet away and out of its escape path. With a wide-angle lens, fully charged strobe, and full roll of film, I shot image after image until I had crawled within an arm's length.

Its gray body glistened like shiny plastic, almost too perfect to be real. Then came the embarrassing awareness that I was the victim of the *Sea*

A HERMIT CRAB PEERS OUT OF his temporary home.

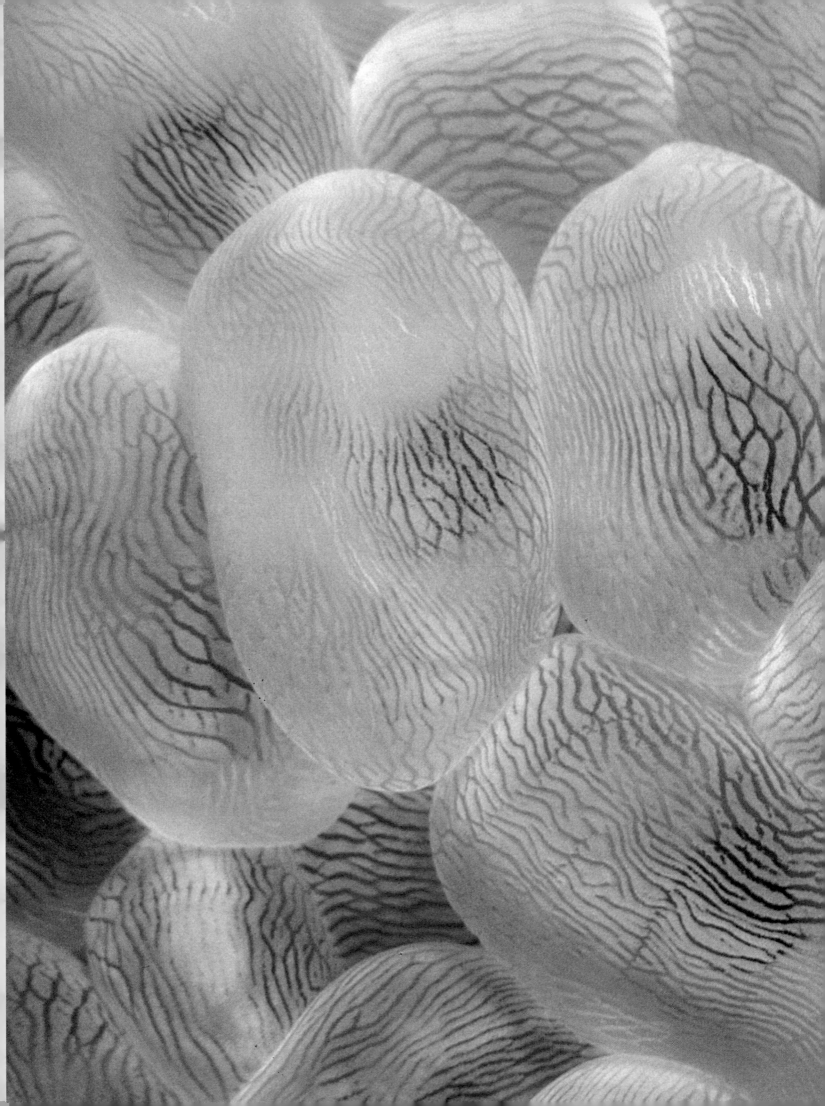

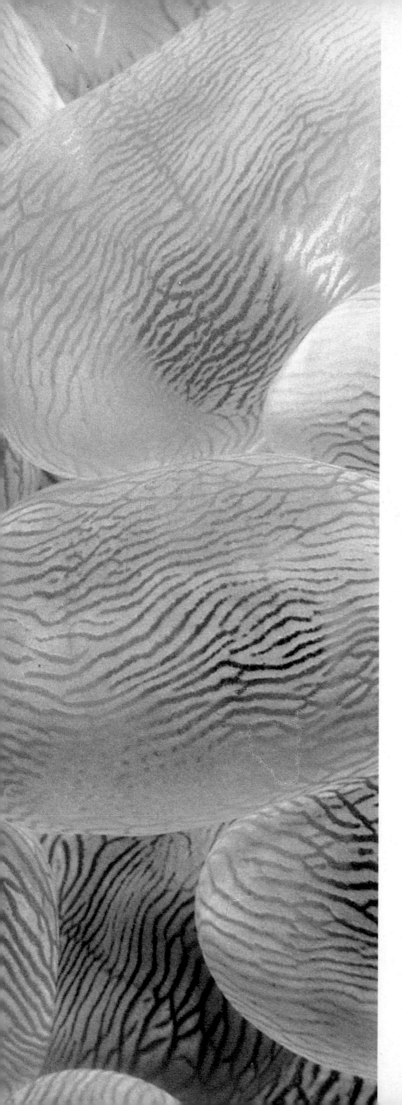

FIJI

143

Fiji isn't a tropical garden of paradise; it just looks and seems that way. Seven hundred thousand Fijians live on one of the largest island groups in the Pacific Ocean. Three hundred sixty islands are scattered over 250,000 square miles of ocean, about two-thirds of the way down a line between Hawaii and New Zealand. Only one hundred of Fiji's islands are permanently inhabited. The others look like they should be, but inadequate supplies of fresh water make them unfit for habitation. They are best suited for coconut palms and other tropical vegetation. The

THE SENSORY TENTACLES OF THIS encrusted bivalve seek out an unsuspecting meal.

Preceding pages:
SEEN IN DAYLIGHT, BUBBLE coral is covered with a host of small, water-filled balloons of tissue that totally obscure its hard skeleton.

Opposite:
ORANGE-FIN ANEMONEFISH ARE generally found in reef passages and outer reef slopes.

largest island, Viti Levu, is the site of the international airport and the capital city of Suva. It is also the third-largest island in the open Pacific, slightly smaller than the island of Hawaii.

Like the Hawaiian Islands, Fiji's geological heritage is volcanic. And like Hawaii, its topography and climate are ideal for growing sugarcane and entertaining tourists, Fiji's two major industries. However, most of the 250,000 tourists who visit each year come from Australia and New Zealand. For some unknown reason, American tourists, especially divers, have overlooked one of the finest resort and diving areas in the world. White sand beaches dot the shorelines. Hundreds of miles of largely unexplored coral reefs weave their way around and between the islands, washed by deep, nutrient-laden, unpolluted waters. The reefs, reef life, and pelagic fishes are stunning.

Fiji is a strikingly beautiful country. Topographically, its islands range from heavily vegetated, mountainous terrain to flat grasslands, from hilly land to flat coral islets. The country enjoys a mild climate, unforgettable sunsets, and people, both Fijian and Indian, who are good-natured and friendly. For divers, the people's warmth will compete with the magnificent beauty of some of the world's most unspoiled and undiscovered coral reefs.

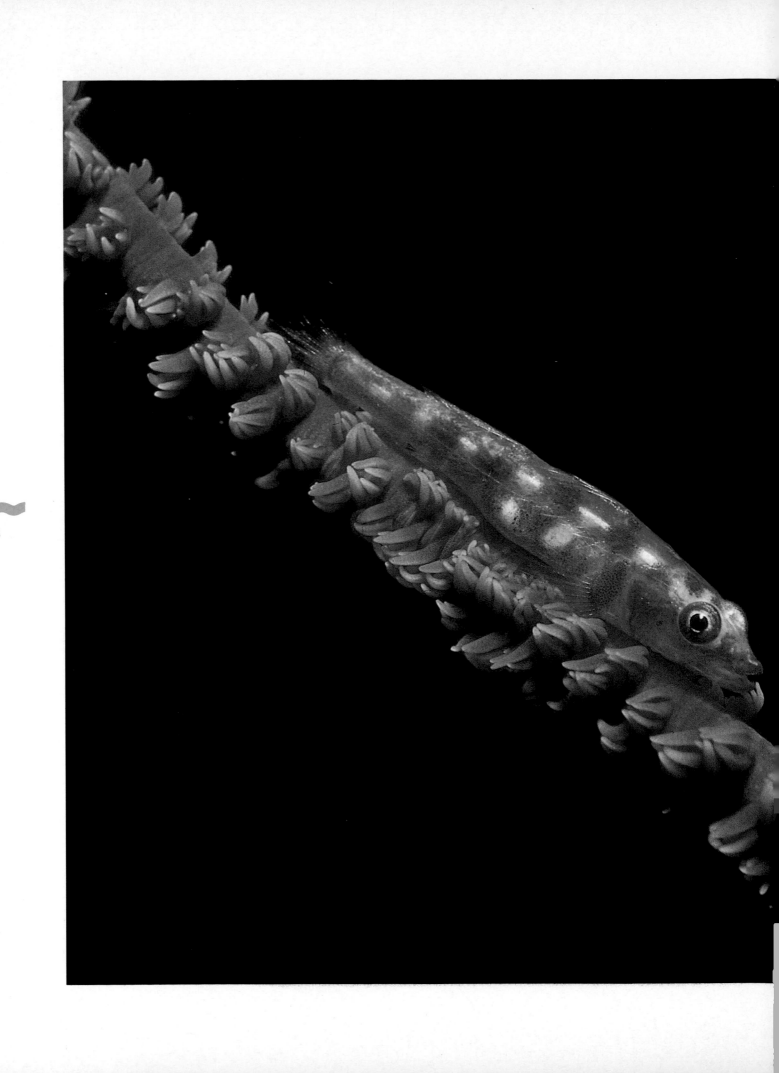

149

CAMOUFLAGING COLORATION
and markings make tiny
blennies hard to see.

One Man, One Vote

From the outset, the electoral system favored the election of an ethnic Fijian-dominated parliament. But in April 1987 when two rival Fijian parties produced a split vote, Indians ended up with a majority and the country had its first Indian prime minister. Within a month, the Fijian army staged a coup and removed the Indian-controlled government. Four months later, the military leadership declared Fiji a republic and affirmed that "the indigenous Fijian race is empowered with the land and right to govern themselves for their advancement and welfare." No mention was made of any rights accruing to the 350,000 ethnic Indians.

Fearing that their economic rights could be expropriated as summarily as their political freedom, many Indian professionals and business owners left Fiji. The country has lost not only their skills, but also their pool of capital. Coupled with the loss of foreign aid, as a result of the coup, from New Zealand, Great Britain, Australia, and the United States, Fiji's economic future is in doubt.

A Slipping Grasp on Tradition

Historically, the Fijians have had an almost pure form of socialism. Communal ownership and sharing of food and village responsibilities worked in a land of plenty; yet that system has gradually changed to a cash economy where people work for wages. Tourism, more than any other factor, has pushed Fiji into a money-based economy rather than one reliant on the basic commodi-

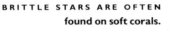

BRITTLE STARS ARE OFTEN found on soft corals.

150

ties of sugarcane and coconuts. Traditionally, the Fijian culture has shown great courtesy towards outsiders. Thus, it isn't accidental that hotels, restaurants, and dive operations are generally staffed by Fijians.

Outwardly, the Fijians are friendly, carefree, and deeply religious. They seem to have been born with smiles on their faces. But these qualities, while genuine, mask a strong nationalism and desire to chart their own destiny as an ethnic people.

The Power Behind Politics

In the last decades of the twentieth century, it's difficult for Americans to comprehend the impact and importance of Fiji's tribal system, an anomaly in the Space Age. Historically, a hierarchical system of both dominance and governance evolved among the warring tribes, with each village's chief as the key figure. In brief, a chiefly pecking order developed that today is embodied in the 150-member Great Council of Chiefs. The council is consulted on all matters of national importance. In fact, the 1987 military coup was instigated by the Great Council of Chiefs; the army simply enforced their wishes.

Even the lowliest of chiefs command respect and power, but not in a flagrant, despotic sense. Rather, the system functions like an organization of unelected American mayors, each of whom personally holds the key to his village. Thus, when the chiefs of Kandavu Island, the site of the famed Astrolabe Reef, believed that scuba divers' bubbles were frightening away the vast schools of reef and pelagic fishes, they suddenly closed the area to divers. Their right to do so was absolute.

Negotiations between the dive operators and island chiefs were conducted through the Great Council of Chiefs. When the operators offered photographic evidence to dispel their fears, the chiefs disbelieved them. How could they be certain where or when the pictures had been taken? During lengthy negotiations, the operators finally convinced the chiefs that bubbles

don't scare fish. The nineteenth-century notion was exploded by twentieth-century technology – the underwater video camera. While bubbles were the excuse, it later became apparent that the underlying issue was economic. The local chiefs resented fishermen from Viti Levu fishing on their reefs, but were powerless to stop what they considered poaching. What they really wanted was greater control over what had once been their absolute domain. Perhaps out of frustration, they demanded – and got – a "head tax" for the privilege of diving on *their* reef.

The power of the chiefs evidences itself in many other ways, some of which I find quite refreshing. Television sets are commonplace in Fiji, but television aerials are not. Pollution-conscious Fijians have, thus far, managed to keep the airwaves clear of television transmission. For now, videos suffice.

Taveuni, a short flight to the northeast of Viti Levu, is known as the "Garden Island" of Fiji. It has lush tropical growth and fertile soil. It is also the site of one of the world's best and smallest dive resorts, Dive Taveuni, and the world-class Rainbow Reef.

Diving logistics are unusual. The boat is moored in the nearest harbor that offers protection from seasonal storms, and getting to it requires a thirty-minute drive. But driving time is well spent seeing and talking about Taveuni island. It took me a couple of days to realize what was so unusual about the natural beauty. The island was pristine and uncluttered. There was no litter, trash or junk along the road, no burial grounds for rusting vehicles, no smoking garbage dumps. It's a beautiful place and the chiefs keep it that way.

GETTING THERE

Getting to and from Fiji is easy, whether from the United States, New Zealand, Australia, or any other major airport around the Pacific Rim. Nandi airport is a hub for international flights. But most domestic flights use Suva's Nausori airport, about 120 miles to the east.

While it's possible to fly to Suva, the three-hour bus ride offers an opportunity to see the sugarcane fields. During the cutting season, miniature narrow-gauge railroad trains are used to haul the cut cane from the fields to the refineries. Tiny steam engines pull long trains of flat cars, mounded high with Fiji's prime commodity. (The sight reminded me of the childhood book *The Little Engine That Could.*) In addition, since the Queen's Road skirts the Coral Coast, we saw the luxury resorts that cater to most tourists. While they all offer diving packages, none are designed for serious divers. Nor are the dive sites comparable to those reached by live-aboard boats. Most are tourist-class, not world-class.

Since return flights to the United States all seem to leave late at night, you will be left with time to kill. The town of Nandi, with its duty-free shops that offer few bargains, is not the place to do it.

Our bus driver suggested we stop at one of the hotels near the airport. What seemed like a con job turned out to be excellent advice. We negotiated day room-rates, had use of the pool, and enjoyed a good dinner. Then the

153

A RAINBOW HAWKFISH, PERCHED
on coral, patiently awaits
unwary prey.

hotel van gave us a free ride to the airport. This procedure was far more preferable than spending seven hours in the crowded and uncomfortable waiting room and snack bar. At least we started the long trip home freshly showered, cleanly clothed, and moderately rested.

WHEN TO GO

For divers, the best time to visit Fiji is April through November (fall through spring). It rains far less, is definitely cooler, and free from the risk of typhoons. In recent years, for some unexplainable reason, these storms have increased in both frequency and magnitude. The trade-off for reduced typhoon risk is more wind during the April – November period, a condition that can and does affect some of the truly great offshore dive sites. Wind-driven waves can make getting in and out of the water difficult. Pitching and rolling boats also make some divers queasy.

VISIT WITH THE PEOPLE

English is the most common spoken language of this polyglot country, followed by Fijian and Hindi. Consequently, Australian, New Zealand, U.S., and other English-speaking tourists find they can converse with virtually any resident Fijian. And this ability to communicate freely is what enhances a tourist's visit, for Fijians are willing to talk with foreigners.

No matter how tight your schedule, make time to visit with the people of Fiji. A few hours spent in one of the numerous native villages will be memorable. Armed with a gift of dried kava roots for the chief (kava is available at any general store), you will be welcomed by a swarm of inquisitive children. Adults hang back initially, but share the friendly curiosity about Americans. And all want their pictures taken. A Polaroid camera will make anyone a celebrity.

The French enjoy a glass of wine, the English thrive on tea, while Americans drink coffee. The Fijian national beverage is kava, prepared from the dried root of a plant in the pepper family. It looks like dishwater and has an indescribable taste reminiscent of an overpeppered cold soup that makes your tongue tingle. Nonalcoholic, it affects people differently, ranging from mild euphoria to numbness in the legs. Serving kava is a sign of hospitality. It is considered rude to refuse the first bowl. After five bowls one night, I walked back to our cabin, slept fitfully, and decided that Fiji Bitter, the local beer, was better.

A MYRIAD OF JEWELS

At the very least, Fiji enjoys five of the world's best diving areas. Yet, few divers have seen them, because they lie beyond the range of land-based

TINY NUDIBRANCHS OCCUR IN an incredible variety of colors and patterns.

155

boats. Furthermore, because Fiji has hundreds of miles of unexplored reefs, no one knows what treasures remain to be found. With two exceptions, the best diving can be experienced only from a live-aboard boat.

Lying between Taveuni and the neighboring island of Vanua Levu is the Somosomo Strait, a double-ended funnel of deep water interrupted at its narrowest point by an underwater shelf called Rainbow Reef. Tidal waters accelerate as they pour over the sill created by the reef, bringing with them a dense concentration of plankton to feed the proliferation of corals and reef fishes. And here, too, is the spectacular and unique "Great White Wall." It is best seen just as the tide turns to bring food to this huge community of white soft corals (*Dendronephthya*) clinging to the sheer reef-face. Why only white soft corals reign over this principality is a mystery. Like a prairie of snow-covered tumbleweed, they extend beyond vision.

At another anchorage, shy court jesters, two tiny blue ribbon eels (*Rhinomuraena quaesita*), with dotted lemon eyes and flared saffron nostrils, peek out from their small holes. Secure in the size of their herd, unicornfish (*Naso unicornis*) graze in the lee of a bommie. Neither the eels nor the unicornfish seem threatened by the presence of divers.

Out of the current in the lee of a small islet, Ric Cammick, owner of Dive

LOOKING MORE LIKE A GIANT flower than an animal, this crimson feather star, its arms coiled, reposes on a sea fan.

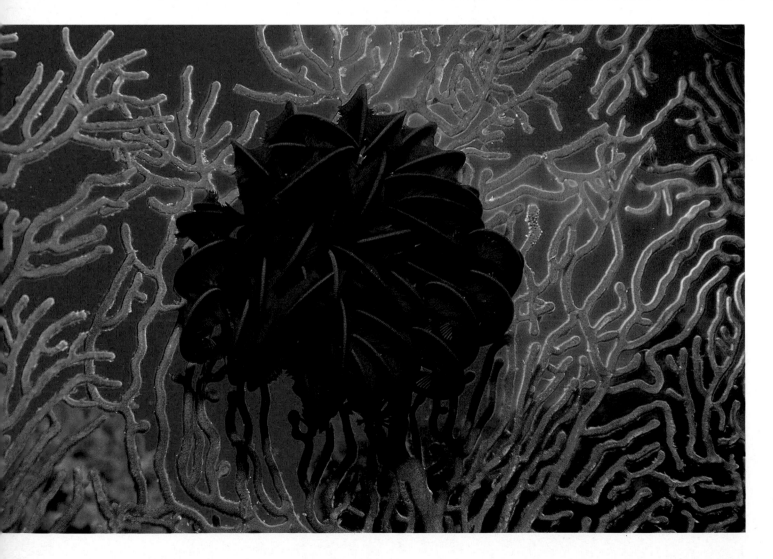

Taveuni, dropped anchor at a place he calls Potpourri, because "it has a little of this and a little of that." The shallow reef was like a sampler except for one thing. It also had the largest concentration of red-and-black anemonefish (*Amphiprion melanopus*) I have ever seen or heard of. Dozens of anemones were tucked into pockets of the table-like stand of staghorn coral, an area roughly twelve-by-twenty feet. The anemonefish popped up or darted down to their hosts somewhat like prairie dogs act when an eagle is soaring over-head. In silhouette, this congregation appeared to be hundreds of tiny, tethered, red-orange balloons bouncing in a breeze.

The dive sites around Mbenga island can also be reached from land. The strait between it and Viti Levu to the north has a funneling effect that creates strong currents and nourishes some magnificent bommies. In over twenty years of diving, we had seen only one clown triggerfish (*Balistoides conspicil-lum*). In the Mbenga Strait, we saw three at once in open water. And lionfish (*Pterois antennata*) were out of their dens and prowling around the bommie walls at midday, not alone but in pairs and trios. On the south side of Mbenga we dove on uncharted patch reefs that teemed with life. We were amazed to find octopus freely roaming about at 10 A.M., in contrast to their usually nocturnal habits. Sea fans, ten feet high, waved like scarlet plumes in the canyons between bommies. Fingernail-sized nudibranchs dotted the brilliantly colored terrain of hard and soft corals. These were dives when we wished for double tanks and seventy-two-exposure rolls of film.

One evening, the chief of Mbenga and two other men motored out to our anchorage, guitars in hand. Wearing the traditional sulus (wraparound skirts) and brilliant T-shirts, they joined the *Pacific Nomad*'s musicians in a concert of Fijian songs—and, of course, the traditional bowl of kava that seemed to fuel everyone's vocal chords. If the normal complement of tourists had filled the big resorts at the time, they would have been on the main island performing their mystical ritual of firewalking. How they can walk across a bed of red-hot stones without injury is a secret known only to this small tribe.

The next afternoon, the divers went ashore to purchase shells from the demure women and smiling children of Mbenga. Such beachfront sales are one of the few sources of cash income for these people. Prices were embarrassingly low and we had been advised to accept them — bargaining is an affront to their dignity.

Kandavu Island is within sight of Mbenga. The Great Astrolabe Reef, named after a nineteenth-century French corvette that was almost wrecked there, extends for eighteen miles to Kandavu's northeast. Inside the lagoon, the water is shallow, thirty to fifty feet deep. But outside, the sheer walls drop more than a mile. Vast schools of pelagic fishes cruise by these walls. Sharks, including the occasionally belligerent bronze whaler (*Carcharinus alenea*), are seen frequently but are usually well beyond photographic range. They are far more intent on the large schools of mackerels and trevally than bubbling divers. These walls are a microcosm of undersea life containing a vast array of colorful corals and gaudily painted fishes.

In contrast, the reef walls around the island of Wakaya are almost devoid of soft corals. But that paucity is balanced by the Tiffany-like showcases of delicate varieties of hard corals, unspoiled by careless divers' fins or typhoons. The omnipresent reef fishes are almost lost in the splendor.

The black-and-white sea krait (*Laticauda*), locally called dadakulaci, is a snake with venom more deadly than the Indian cobra. It lays terrestrial eggs and must leave the water to reproduce. Yet, in Fiji these sea snakes have long been a children's plaything and considered harmless. Perhaps because the snake's head is small and its venom-inducing teeth are at the rear of its jaw (rather than at the front like pit vipers), there is no record of anyone having been bitten. Nevertheless, they are still potentially deadly.

For truly venturesome divers, a rare opportunity has developed to explore a vast area of virgin reefs, the Lau group, a scattering of volcanic and coral islands, located at the easternmost extremity of Fiji across the Koro Sea. This is almost an expedition in itself due to the remote location. However, Marine Pacific, Ltd., the owners of *Pacific Nomad*, have scouted the territory and worked out the logistics. Travel will be more time-consuming, but once the ship anchors at Lau, divers will experience some of Fiji's rarest jewels.

WHAT MAKES FIJI SPECIAL?

The Fiji archipelago is one of many idyllic island groups in the tropical Pacific. Like the others, it is a scattering of lush green dots set in an azure sea, with marvelous coral gardens and dramatic dropoffs at its doorstep. The seas teem with tropical reef fishes and an abundance of marine invertebrates—and, to make sure diving stays exciting, occasional large pelagics, such as manta rays, sweep along the wall. As is typical of the tropical Pacific, giant sea anemones, with symbiotic clownfish in attendance, are familiar sights, as are feathery-armed crinoids of many hues. Gaudily colored nudibranchs are easily found; gigantic orange-yellow sea fans protrude from the walls; and massive tridacna clams, with mantles of rainbow colors and designs, are also common. Deadly lionfish ruffle feathery fins in their hideaways on the reef; and the number of species of butterflyfish fluttering about is quite astonishing.

In Fiji, one of my favorite dives is in a "pass"—a narrow canyon leading from a lagoon behind the reef to the open water along the wall outside. Passes are especially exciting because of the action encountered there. They act as giant funnels moving food in and out of the lagoon with the current created by the changing tides. During outflowing tides, sharks, schools of barracuda, large groupers, and other predators wait near the entrance to see what might be swept out in the current. Inflowing tides are a treat as the water coming from the open seas is often crystal clear. As you near the entrance, the current increases, catching you in one of the most dramatic of drift dives. Effortlessly you glide by great coral heads, while schools of jacks and other fish approach, attracted by your bubbles. The speed heightens as the canyon narrows, and you may find yourself zooming along at a full three to four knots. Coral gardens whiz by below, displaying breathtaking beauty and variety. The wonderful adventure ends as you enter the shallow lagoon.

Yet drift dives in passes and abundant marine life are

· MANY OF FIJI'S REEFS HAVE NEVER BEEN ·
seen by divers. (Carl Roessler)

not unique to Fiji alone. What distinguishes this island spot in my mind from other dive destinations are three things in particular. First on my list are the soft corals, especially around Taveuni and Astrolabe Reef. The soft corals can be found in nearly every color—but the red ones are particularly striking, seeming to be everywhere and coming in all shades of red. The vermilion ones are astonishing! Strobe shots of these corals guarantee "oohs" and "aahs" from viewers. At the Great White Wall out of Taveuni is an area in about a hundred feet of water where nothing but glowing,

V I G N E T T E   B Y   P A U L   H U M A N N

bluish-white soft corals grow as far as the eye can see. Slowly cruising along this wall is like taking a trip into some sort of dreamland.

· PHYLLIDS ARE NUDIBRANCHS THAT POSSESS NUMEROUS GILLS ·
along the edges of their half-thumb-sized bodies.

A second thing that makes Fiji outstanding is its great gardens of hard corals—especially those in the Lau group of islands. No place in the Pacific can match them. For miles, crowding every square inch of substrata are healthy corals of all descriptions and colors, each fighting for its own growing space. While small areas in other places may rival these gardens, never are there vast expanses like this—ones that seem to go on forever.

And thirdly, an important aspect of any trip—the people. Fijians are simply the friendliest folks I have ever encountered. On a drive into the backcountry of Viti Levu, the main island, I almost got tired of waving and shouting their greeting: "Bulla!" You always feel good about a place when

you believe you are genuinely welcome.

Yes, Fiji is one of the world's great dive destinations—a wonderful place that all divers should put on their list.

· NOT SURPRISINGLY, THIS ALGAE IS COMMONLY CALLED GREEN ·
grape algae.

· CHRISTMAS-TREE WORMS OCCUR IN MANY COLORS AND ·
patterns; no one knows why.

PAPUA
NEW GUINEA

163

Papua New Guinea is the wreckage of a massive accident involving five, maybe six, slow-moving participants in a continuing cataclysm that started hundreds of millions of years ago — a collision of tectonic plates. Unlike the sideswipe that created the Sea of Cortez or the bumper-locking that made the Red Sea fall, this was a massive fender bender.

Originally, the southern terrain of the island of New Guinea was part of Australia's northern continental shelf, flat and submerged most of the time. It was the leading edge of the northern-moving Indian-Australian

Preceding pages:
FEW PLACES IN THE WORLD
offer divers the opportunity to
see such a profusion of fishes.

plate, quite tranquil until the other plates entered the arena from the north and east. The initial crashes generated such earth-wrenching friction that volcanic action tossed up an arc of islands where none had been.

Riding on their Pacific plate hosts, these islands drifted toward the inevitable smash with Australia. Then, maybe twenty million years ago, the colossal collision occurred. The oceanic crust of the westernmost islands were torn, twisted, wrinkled, and piled onto Australia's leading edge, welded together by the incredible heat. Smoldering volcanoes dimple the line of impact. Still grinding, the tectonic plates even now send earthquake quivers through the wreckage of modern New Guinea. When the cataclysm created the world's second-largest island, it also made it one of the most unstable geologic areas.

From outer space, New Guinea seems to roost on the northernmost tip of Australia, like a giant green prehistoric bird with seemingly more spine and ribs than meat. Over a century ago, politicians severed the tail end from the head. With an ink line along the 141st meridian, the head and breast became part of what is now Indonesia. The hind end and tail, along with six hundred islands and uncountable islets, became Papua New Guinea in 1975 when

Australia relinquished administrative control to an independent and freely elected government.

A Topographical Textbook

Papua New Guinea is a geographer's galaxy of topographical features. The unique combination has created such a prolific marine environment that PNG is one of the best areas in the world for scuba diving.

Eighty percent of the area encompassed by its borders is tropical water. In fact, only the boundary with Irian Jaya, Indonesia, falls on dry land. All others are compass bearings, invisible lines on the Bismarck Sea, the Equator, the Solomon Sea, and the Coral Sea. While these borders surround an area the size of Mexico, the land mass comprises less than one-fourth of the total. The country is a sparsely populated, rural, agrarian society. Less than 10 percent of its 3 million people live in cities.

Whether approaching from sea or air, visitors are struck by the diversity of the terrain. Coastlines vary from huge expanses of mangrove swamp, marshland, and jungle to palm-fringed white sand beaches. Precipitous, verdant cliffs, which are sometimes the walls of dormant or active volcanoes, drop into the sea. Inland, the terrain can turn into rolling expanses of savannah grassland, eucalyptus woods, or forested foothills. And everywhere on the main island and most of the large outer islands the land slopes upward steeply. Mountains are the predominant feature of Papua New Guinea.

From the Irian Jaya border to the tip of Milne Bay, mountain ranges interweave and interlock to form a barrier between the north and south coasts so formidable that no roads cross the country and so high that planes must pick their way through cloud-covered mountain passes. Many of the peaks exceed 10,000 feet in height; the highest, Mt. Wilhelm, is 15,400 feet. Imagine diving in 85°F. water on a clear day and being within eyesight of ice-covered mountaintops!

This, the largest chain of mountains between the Himalayas and the Andes, lies on an east-west axis, the perfect orientation for blocking the prevailing winds and causing rain, a lot of rain. Any weatherman who predicted rainfall daily in PNG would be batting 1,000. Generally speaking, the climate is hot, humid, and rainy.

However, those conditions vary widely depending on location and/or season. For example, one morning we left our mosquito-netted beds at the Karawari Lodge in the jungles of the northwest to fly to Tari in the Southern Highlands. That night we slept under down comforters at the Ambua Lodge, seven thousand feet higher but only ninety miles south. Although it was the rainy season in both locations, we never got wet, because it usually pours at night. For divers who want to get soaked but not seasick, diveable waters can *always* be found, because the dry season conveniently shifts around the shores, islands, and reefs. This explains why live-aboard boats offer varying, seasonal itineraries.

But the mountains and rainfall have several other implications for divers traveling in PNG. Fueled by year-round downpours and fertile soil, the flora

A CURIOUS CRAB INSPECTS
a sponge.

168

the inability to converse in a country with 732 separate languages. Papua New Guinea was and still is a time warp, a mecca for anthropologists and a must for curious divers.

A CHANGING CULTURE

Missing the opportunity to visit the Highlands or Sepik River area would be like making two dives a day when you could do four or five. While tour guides tend to show visitors the staged glitter of tribal reenactments in local villages, the brilliantly painted bodies of amateur actors do not obscure the humdrum reality of everyday living. The native guides provided us by Trans Niugini Tours also took us into villages that would have been otherwise inaccessible. Thus, in addition to historical rituals, we also experienced life as it is lived — and that is very basic. The quest for food, clothing, and shelter supersede the frivolities of modern man.

The essential element required to gain access to this still primitive society is the entree provided by a guide who speaks the local languages. Tour groups are small and highly personalized. With a guide and a four-wheel-drive vehicle or flat-bottomed river boat, you can go practically anywhere. It

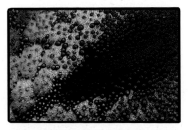

**A DETAILED LOOK AT PART
of a soft tree coral colony.**

is an experience well worth the expense – which is not inconsiderable.

An equal rights amendment is about as remote from PNG as any place in the world. In this rural, subsistence society, women are responsible for tending the gardens, pigs, and children in that order. (Pigs are both a form of currency and, more importantly, a measure of wealth and prestige). Girls and women cook, cut firewood, and weave mats and thatching.

On the other hand, men tend to specific tasks like building houses, clearing land for gardens, making canoes, hunting small game, and fishing. But, in the ten-or-so villages we visited, we observed groups of men and boys sitting around and talking or playing bingo. Occasionally, men revert to their age-old custom of warring with neighboring villages, with bow and arrows the preferred weapon. They don't perceive murder as a crime but rather as a way of life (a custom that missionaries and the central government have been trying hard to change). Death begets retaliation, à la Hatfield and McCoy.

Relatives of a murder victim are obliged to avenge his death so that his wandering spirit may rest. But the "payback," as the custom is called, does not require retaliation against the actual murderer. Any member of his clan or village will suffice. In February 1988, we witnessed a funeral gathering, the result of a "payback" and evidence of a culture still in transition.

Contrasts are everywhere. One evening at a first-class hotel in Port Moresby, we watched the winter olympics via live satellite coverage – yet most villages have no electricity, much less television sets. A few nights later, we were anchored in a beautiful bay at the eastern end of the main island. Our boat was surrounded by villagers in canoes straining for a view of the movie playing on the boat's television. Firelight danced over black water.

Hurdling Language Barriers

In a country still dominated by tribalism instead of nationalism, one of the few common denominators is the official language, English. The adoption of

SEEN IN CLOSE-UP, A SEA anemone poses on a red sea fan.

a "foreign" national language was a concession to the difficulty of choosing among the seven-hundred-plus native tongues – since even the most predominant native language has fewer than 35,000 practitioners. Fortunately for English-speaking tourists, English is spoken almost everywhere.

Hurdling the Mountains, Rivers and Seas

For the most part, travelers do not see traffic jams. In fact, they don't see many roads either, especially in the mountainous interior and river basins. Road systems are local, not national. Paved roadways are, with rare exception, very local. PNG is one of the few countries in the world where the capital is isolated from every other major city, and it may always be so. For even if the money were available to build roads, bridges, and tunnels, the unstable earth, torrential rains, and rugged terrain make road building and maintenance an engineer's nightmare. Consequently, Papua New Guinea has become a country laced together with invisible air paths.

LIKE FLOWERS REACHING FOR the sun, soft corals wave in the breeze of ocean current.

A MAGNIFIED VIEW OF A SEA cucumber's skin.

Airplanes are the vehicle of nationalism. Although the terrain and un-predictable local weather conditions make flying precarious at times, the national air safety record is admirable. Perhaps this is due to the government requirement concerning visual flight rules. Generally, pilots must be able to see where they are going. Instrument and night landings simply don't happen on most domestic flights. Unfortunately, the cost of delivering this service is high. Fares on the national airlines make travel costs elsewhere seem cheap.

A Stable Government

For a Third World country that gained independence only in 1975, PNG is remarkably progressive and politically stable. It has weathered several changes of government yet maintained a strong and viable parliamentary system. And while rival politicians differ widely on policies, they have been careful to maintain the independence of the press and the individual rights of free speech and assembly.

Of course, they are all too aware that the PNG economy relies heavily upon annual grants of foreign aid from Australia. The mutual best interests of both countries revolve around the sustained growth of a democratic, free-market economy in PNG.

Fortunately, PNG has vast deposits of copper and gold that make it less dependent on its agricultural exports of coffee, copra, and cocoa. The Depart-ment of Minerals and Energy estimates that PNG has all the potential to

AN UNIDENTIFIED BLENNY.

become the world's third-largest producer of gold within ten years.

Like many countries, PNG maintains a 200-mile fishing zone around its landmass. Fortunately for divers, the government has taken a hard-nosed attitude toward foreign fishing fleets and poachers. This stance undoubtedly contributes to the profusion and diversity of pelagic fishes seen by divers.

GETTING THERE

Flying to and from the edge of discovery requires careful planning and coordination between two or more airlines. It is a task best left to travel agents. Both the sheer distance and connecting flights in Port Moresby are the stumbling blocks. Domestic flights tend to leave in the early A.M., but no international flights arrive until later. Thus, tourists are destined to spend a night in the least desirable spot in the whole country.

Port Moresby is both the capital and gateway to PNG. The city sprawls over hills and valleys and around many bays. It is the hub of shipping, banking, commerce, air transport, government, and manufacturing. Port Moresby is also the center of unemployment. The large population of idle young men has caused a national embarrassment, widespread burglary, and sidewalk robbery.

Only the poorest dwellings and shops aren't surrounded by chain-link fences topped with barbed wire. Gates, grates, and steel bars adorn doors and windows. Wrought iron is functional, not ornamental. Even the best hotels employ security systems. Guests are cautioned by the government to place valuables in safe-deposit boxes and to stay off the streets at night. Port Moresby is a good place to leave!

SOME HELPFUL HINTS

Even if you're not an avid photographer, bring a camera and more film than you think you'll need. Film is very expensive and selection is limited. A telephoto lens will capture facial expressions that are priceless. Incidentally, you don't have to pay people to take their picture. They like to be photographed. A Polaroid camera and a free hand with giveaways will make you popular with all ages everywhere.

Coupled with the joys of travelling in this fascinating country is the responsibility for personal health. Malaria is a fact of life in PNG. Visitors are advised by local and international health officials to take a prophylactic anti-malarial drug. Since mosquitoes other than the species that carries malaria can also be bothersome at times, bring the strongest repellant you can buy.

PNG requires a thirty-day visa for U.S. citizens. Visas are readily available at the Port Moresby airport for a nominal fee, 5 kina, and a three-minute wait. Australia also requires visas of all U.S. citizens. However, if you are in transit, have a valid passport, on-going plane ticket, and no more than a forty-

REEFS TEEM WITH LIFE.

eight hour layover, no visa is required. You just fill out some forms at the airport.

Finally, Air Niugini is stingy with baggage allowances. Officially, domestic passengers are entitled to 20kg (44 pounds) each. Divers are allowed an additional 16kg (35 + pounds). With cameras, no diver could make the allowance. Consequently, our group of five was advised to place the five heaviest dive bags in a separate pile and *tell* the check-in clerks that those bags were diving equipment and, therefore, free. The clerks were so confused with all the other bags, weights, and tickets that they agreed. Considering the airfares charged and the official posture of encouraging foreign divers, no one got cheated.

THE HIGH COST OF TOURISM

UNLIKE MOST ANEMONEFISHES, the pink anemonefish's diet consists mainly of benthic algae.

If there is any negative associated with diving in PNG, it is the cost. Faced with the prospects of declining grants from Australia and a still immature economy, the government has imposed heavy duties on the imported foods, meats, and equipment that foreign divers expect. For example, all diving

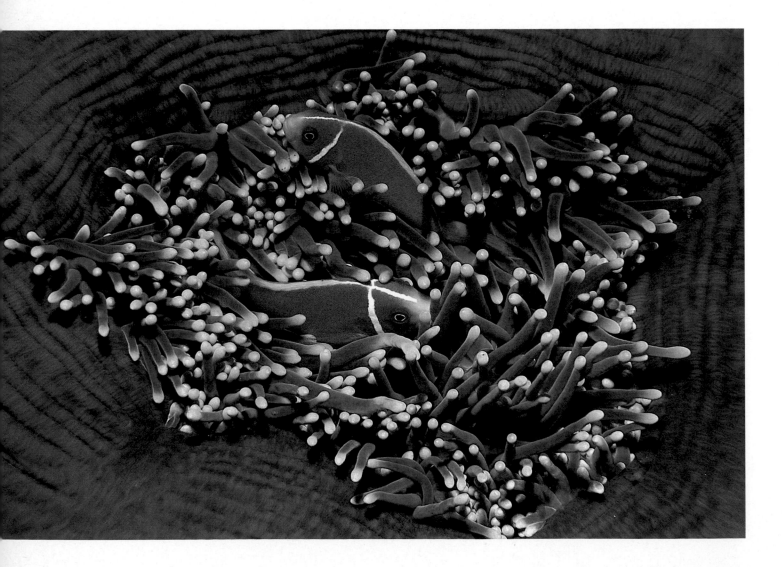

equipment, including compressors and spare parts, carries a 25 percent tariff. Shipping costs are high, because the country imports so much and exports so little. Hotels import building materials, furniture, and fixtures. The government-owned airline buys foreign aircraft, aviation fuel from Singapore, and employs pilots from Australia and New Zealand. Faced with these economic realities and what many consider an artificially high value of the local currency, the dollar simply doesn't buy very much. The only good news is that tipping is not customary — although we chose to tip the crew of our live-aboard dive boat. Costs are astronomical, but the diving is astral!

AN UNDERWATER GOLD MINE

If you could count the stars under the Southern Cross, maybe you could count the nuggets of life under the Solomon and Bismarck Seas. Nowhere else in the world have we seen so many species and nowhere else have we seen such profusion of animal life. For wreck enthusiasts, the abundance of World War II ships and aircraft, both Japanese and American, rivals the Ghost Fleet of Truk Lagoon. Diving conditions range from placid to strenuous. Water temperatures are in the tepid eighties. PNG diving is lavish and diverse. The good news is that there is so much to see. The sad news is that even on a month-long trip, no one could completely sample the diversity. Six of our contributing photographers have travelled to PNG, some on numerous and extended occasions — none have captured the same images.

Only one condition prevents me from presenting an Oscar to Papua New Guinea. The planktonic "soup" that feeds this fabulous ecosystem also clouds visibility, sometimes down to forty feet. Yes, there are sites with water as gin-clear as the Red Sea or Marion Reef, but they are in the minority. The trade-off for seeing a huge school of giant barracuda is not being able to see it all in one glance.

LEVIATHANS OF THE DEEP

The likelihood of seeing big animals is far greater than mere chance. For some, like killer whales and schooling hammerhead sharks, probability is affected by season. But in one ten-day cruise aboard the *Telita* around the eastern tip, or Milne Bay area, of the main island, we saw enough big animals to overstock the largest aquarium in the world.

As we were anchoring on the brink of a 600-fathom wall fifty yards off the jungled shore, a whale shark surfaced. By the time we got into the "soup," the giant plankton-eater was gone. Once in the water, we flippered back and forth along the top of the wall, about fifty feet deep. All we saw was a trio of pygmy mantas (*Mobula diabolus*), distinguished from their namesake by head fins that curve outward, mouths placed much lower on their bodies, and their smaller, ten-foot width. The white tip reef sharks were small by comparison. We were so fascinated by the pea green, four-foot disc sponges that we almost missed the acrobatic contortions of the ten-foot hammerhead as he

DESPITE THEIR FEARSOME REP-
utation, barracuda give divers a
wide berth.

slashed his way through a huge school of Pedley's fusiliers beneath the boat.

Later that day we dove on a patch reef farther up the coast. We had been amused by the antics of a large school of unicorn surgeon fish (*Naso brevirostris*), a fish considered rare in most of the world but common in PNG. The fish were nervous, frequently breaking formation, but generally holding to one location. Yet, the white tip and gray reef sharks cruising the reef's edge had not attacked or threatened them. With our air supply getting low, five of us hung on the anchor chain at thirty feet, hoping for one more chance to review the regiment of giant barracuda we had seen earlier. Air nearly exhausted, we broke through the four-foot surface layer of translucent plankton to be greeted by the excited shouts of the others onboard. "Did you see it? It was huge!" They were more excited than the unicorn fish. "Did we see *what*?" we asked. "A twelve-foot tiger shark [*Galeocerdo cuvieri*] circling the boat!" Only the divers didn't know the slow-moving man-eater was within thirty feet. If we had, I suspect we would have also perfected walking on water.

Visions of giant green and hawksbill turtles compete with those of the refrigerator-sized, chameleon-like brown spotted cod. But are these images better than seeing two ten-foot dugong cows with calves on their backs?

BANANA BOMMIE

Only once in twenty-nine years of underwater adventures have I come to the surface and written down what I saw. Banana Bommie, an exposed patch reef swept by a swift surface current, was the place. I simply could not believe so many fishes could inhabit such a pocket-sized reef. Immense schools of king fish, jacks, goatfish, trevally, and fusiliers patiently sliced through the shoals of bait fishes, seemingly oblivious to the several species of sharks cruising their flanks. Solitary dogtooth tuna patrolled for stragglers. A vast field of

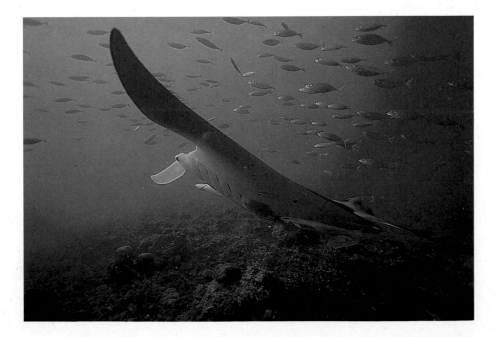

A MANTA RAY TAKES FLIGHT.

garden eels watched from below. Three species of lionfish openly fluttered about great stands of black coral. Tucked in and around the corals were schools of basslets — blue, orange, purple, and yellow blurs. Angelfish and butterfly fishes strutted the ramps, competitors in a beauty contest with sweetlips, coral trout, blennies, rabbitfish, and latticed monocle bream. A blue-spotted fantail ray waited patiently for the evening's swimsuit contest. Film in two cameras was exhausted far before the possibilities.

MOST BLENNIES ARE LESS than two inches long, which makes them difficult to see.

AN ARRAY OF ANEMONEFISHES

Perhaps PNG's strategic location between the Indian and Pacific Oceans caused the largest aggregation of anemonefishes in the world. Nine of twenty-five species are found there, along with domino damselfish (*Dascyllus trimaculatus*), the alien squatters who also have perfected the technique of living among anemones' stinging tentacles. Since anemonefishes are considered delicacies by many reef predators such as groupers, they don't survive away from their hosts. However, since their larvae are pelagic for periods of two to three weeks before they exercise squatter's rights on an unoccupied

ALWAYS FOUND IN PAIRS, THE uncommon fire goby maintains a head up position near its burrow.

UNICORN FISH ARE EASILY
distinguished by the unicorn-
like "horn" on their foreheads.
(Stephen Frink)

182

anemone, I suspect this congregation of species is the result of an evolution-ary reef-hopping done by their minute larvae over eons. Whatever the reason, there are more species here than anywhere else.

NIGHT DIVER'S DELIGHT

One hundred feet from shore and slightly farther from the mouth of a small river, Bob Halstead, one of the best-known and most knowledgeable dive operators in PNG, anchored the *Telita* for a night dive. In twenty feet of murky water over a muddy, detritus-covered bottom, it was a most unlikely spot for diving of any sort.

Standing on the bottom photographing a trio of squid, my spotting light revealed a tiny orange reflection from the silt. Closer inspection showed the pyramid-like etchings on the orange, brown, and white enamel of a textile cone (*Conus textile*). These animals have inflicted serious and occasionally fatal wounds on unsuspecting humans who picked up a "pretty" shell but didn't know it was as lethal as a similar-sized handgrenade.

Ounce for ounce, cone shells are among the most deadly creatures found on reefs. Slow-moving bottom dwellers, these small molluscs don't want to become specimens in shell collections. Rather, they want to be left alone to hunt and to kill, something at which they are very good.

Cones hunt at night, by scent. Once the unsuspecting prey is within inches, the cone brings its magazine-loaded harpoon or radula into play. With a speed uncharacteristic of its snail's pace, it stabs its victim (usually another species of shelled mollusc), which dies almost instantly from the highly toxic venom and is slowly devoured.

Eyes now focused on the bottom, we swam into deeper water. Nothing but silty sand until our lights picked up the tiny, twinkling lights of some-thing resembling an alien spaceship. Only six inches in diameter, the fire urchin (*Asthensoma varium*) has hundreds of short, venom-tipped spines reflecting pinpoints of yellow, gold, and bright blue, all patterned around its orange, seemingly glowing, body. But why does this nocturnal urchin have such exquisitely beautiful markings, visible best under the brilliant strobe light of the lucky photographer?

A BOMBER NAMED "BLACK JACK"

Just off the beach of a place called Cape Vogel in southeastern New Guinea lies the intact wreckage of an American B–17 bomber named *Black Jack*. The plane sits on a patch of flat sand just large enough to safely cradle its 104-foot wingspan and 75-foot length. Ragged coral reefs and twenty-five fathoms of water have protected it since July 11, 1943, when the plane and its crew of ten crash-landed.

After making a night bombing run on the Japanese airfield at Rabaul, 370 miles to the northeast, two of its four engines failed. Then, while buffeted by heavy winds and rain, the aircraft's gyrocompass failed. The plane was hopelessly lost in clouds, its fuel running low. The pilot's only option was to drop down out of the clouds and attempt to ditch the plane in the sea. Strong wind gusts blew the plane just beyond the shallow fringing reef that protected the village of Boga Boga. All ten crewmen escaped into life rafts as the B–17 sank. But the winds blew the awkward rafts away from the beach. To the villagers, the event was incomprehensible. However, they quickly decided to rescue the men in the strange yellow canoes. All survived.

THIS STRIKINGLY BEAUTIFUL fire urchin prowls around shallow, sandy bottoms at night. (Robert Boye)

183

The wreckage of the *Black Jack* was lost and forgotten until 1986 when a group of Australian ex-fliers and scuba divers came to PNG in search of one of their own planes that had also crash-landed. Their hunt led them to Boga Boga and an old man named Valentine who remembered the incident of forty-three years earlier when the white men had crashed into the sea on the giant, noisy bird. With Valentine's help, the Australians quickly located the plane. Of course, it was not the Australian plane that they were hoping to find. But in the spirit of military brotherhood, they identified the wreck and eventually even tracked down its American pilot. And, too, their efforts located this eerily awesome museum piece so that other divers can share their thrill of discovery. Even at 155 feet, the dive is well worth making.

OPEN-ARMED HOSPITALITY

One of the great joys of diving for us is the anticipation of discovery, seeing something for the first time. Cuttlefish (*Solitosepia liliani*) aren't rare, it's just that we had never seen one of these two-foot-long, ten-tentacled cousins of the octopus and squid. By expanding or contracting the chromatophores in their flesh, they can rapidly change color and pattern to blend with their shallow reef background. Extremely good eyesight enables them to see their prey of fish or crustaceans. Their well-developed brains and amazing bursts of speed enable them to capture elusive prey. By squeezing water out of their mantles through omnidirectional siphons, they can change direction on a dime. We were fascinated by their curiosity and by their willingness to let us approach so closely. But then, perhaps they were studying us more intently than we were them.

Of the few shelled cephalopods that have survived the eons, the chambered nautilus (*Nautilus pompilius*) is legendary—known for its shell that when neatly bisected longitudinally reveals an engineering marvel of both form and function, a spiral of ever-increasing whorls. But divers rarely see the living animal, because its habitat is far deeper than even decompression depths. Thus, to photograph one, we invaded its territory with a baited trap set at fifty fathoms. Because the nautilus's chambers also provide the ultimate form of buoyancy compensator, its brief but rapid trip to the surface did not endanger its life, only its privacy. A siphonal tube that extends through a small hole in all the chamber walls enables it to control the amount of gas in each. Consequently, it can rise or sink as it chooses.

As soon as it broke the surface, we took it back down to seventy feet where it regained its equilibrium. Unlike the squid and cuttlefish, its ten-tentacled cousins, the nautilus may have as many as ninety appendages protruding from the open end of its six-inch shell. Each tentacle has a retractable, feeler-like extension, which gives the nautilus prodigious adhesive power, whether to cling to a wall or a hapless fish. Clearly, we had taken this gentle, slow-moving jewel out of its deep-water element. But equally as clearly, we too were swimmers in an alien environment. After fifteen minutes of wonderment, we let the nautilus continue its downward drift.

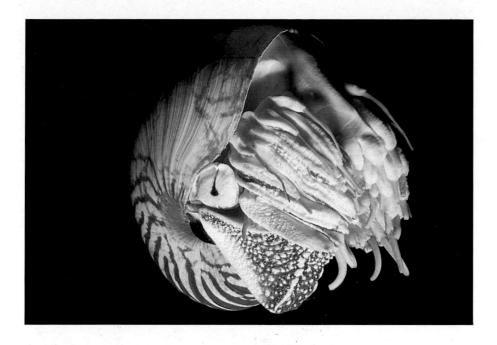

EPILOGUE

Inevitably, we ask ourselves whether our presence in this primitive, pristine part of the world damages the essence of what we came to see and to experience. Marty Snyderman relates how he once was at the Tari airport in the Southern Highlands waiting for a plane. A barefooted man approached, wearing a string loincloth. He was also wearing an old suit jacket over his bare chest. One of the Huli tribe, famed for their prowess in battle and their intricate wigs adorned with bird of paradise feathers, he wore a St. Louis Cardinal baseball cap and carried a briefcase. Marty followed him into the airport building where the man proceeded to unlock and operate the reservations computer behind the counter. Struck by the improbability of the scene, Marty recalls: "In a way, I felt like I didn't have the right to be there. But my not being there wouldn't stop the rapid progress of change."

Just as many once-pristine, unexplored parts of the world such as PNG are going through processes of change, so the undersea environment that the diver explores is fragile and evolving. I think back to the islands of the Caribbean and remember the imprint that humans have left in the underwater world; or to the Great Barrier Reef and the Sea of Cortez where the changes we can observe have been wrought through the forces of nature — obviously with some help from humans. Nature has built an amazing and complete ecosystem, dazzling to the eye, one we are just beginning to know, one that balances itself through its own self-regulation. At Truk Lagoon, for example, the scars and detritus of war have been transformed into natural wonders.

Sport divers have the opportunity to observe the underwater evolution of perfection and beauty, to see the best of what remains while leaving only their bubbles behind. Yet, we as divers also have the responsibility for the safekeeping of these jewels. By protecting our undersea legacy, we can preserve it for generations to come.

PAPUA NEW GUINEA

I f there is a terrestrial equivalent to the underwater wilds of New Guinea, it has long since vanished, fallen victim to the pressures of advancing civilization. Perhaps the Africa of a century ago came closest, before its vast wildlife treasures were decimated. But now the mighty lion, king of the jungle, raises his eyes only to stare, bored, into the reflection of one hundred telephoto lenses protruding from a herd of safari vans.

The sea, however, has been able to hide her favorite children still, offering protection that the land has failed to give. Happily there remain some jewels in this crown of na-

· A BANDED CORAL SHRIMP PREPARES TO CLEAN PARASITES ·
from a normally aggressive brown-flecked reef eel.

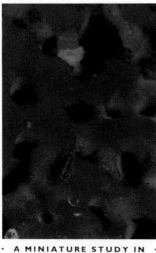

· A MINIATURE STUDY IN ·
green and orange

ture, places where the imprint of Man has had little impact. And among these gems, one shines with greater brilliance than all the rest. This is Papua New Guinea.

Here, steaming volcanic mountains cloaked in capes of lush foliage thrust upward from the blue waters. Jungle birds call from their roosts on the slopes, while threads of smoke rise from clusters of thatched-roof huts along the shore. As our dive boat anchors, crude dugout canoes slip from the beach, and paddlers of all ages surround us, quiet, staring, wide-eyed, curious. They shyly accept our gifts of candy with smiles as wide as the Pacific, their teeth stained deep red with betelnut juice. The silence suddenly erupts with their giggles and excited, joyous chatter, while birds, not to be outdone, burst into chaotic song. Then all falls quiet once again.

There is a primal energy here, underwater—raw, wild, untouched. As I turn to the reef, a school of fish seems to explode, like thunder behind my back. Startled, I spin around to see dozens of large jacks racing through a cloud of

VIGNETTE BY CHRIS NEWBERT

· A CLOSE-UP LOOK AT THE MOUTH OF AN ANEMONE. ·

· THIS SPECIES OF SEA ANEMONE TOTALLY ENVELOPS ITS PREY. ·

ful rhythm, and peace is restored. Tiny reef fish forage among the labyrinthine umbrella of corals, oblivious to the commotion above, preoccupied, it would appear, by showing off their gaudy dress. And, not unlike the volcanos that ring these lagoons, gigantic barrel sponges thrust upward, like huge monoliths, like Easter Island sculptures, formed over a million years of evolution. Soft corals strain at their bases, evidence of an increase in tidal current. The pace of the reef quickens. Survival instincts are placed on alert, a collective adrenaline flows all around. A patrol of 200-pound tuna passes overhead. They must be thirty in number. Then, incautiously, a smaller fish strays from its school, to attempt an easy meal among the rich flow of nutrients carried by the tide. A single tuna reacts with blinding speed, launching itself like a missile: instantly the fish disappears. At once the reef is an orgy of collisions, as if this was the starting whistle of an undersea rugby match. Several larger silver-tip sharks appear, scattering their smaller, more contentious cousins; they themselves remain relaxed with that self-assured confidence that only such masters of an environment can achieve. Their presence is calming, as if the entire reef were hypnotized by the graceful, lazy sweep of their huge tails. Within seconds, the chaos subsides, but an electricity remains, slowly building once again, waiting for the next bolt to strike. We had never dived here before. In fact, no one had. It was a chance selection and we are perhaps the first ever to see this reef. Tens of thousands of years in the making, a wildlife showcase beyond one's imagination, but until this day, until this very moment, hidden from the eyes of man.

187

fusiliers. Panic in their ranks, their disciplined formation now a shambles, suddenly the fusiliers are fewer in number, tentatively reforming as the jacks disappear into the blue. Elsewhere, a swirling school of barracuda sets a more grace-

This is Papua New Guinea.

INDEX

189

190

To the jewels in my life:
Nancy, my best friend,
lover, and only dive
buddy for thirty years;
Kristen, Whitney, Kathryn,
Sarah, Gordon, and Melina,
the gems in our family
bracelet

Editor: Robert Morton
Designer: Stephanie Bart-Horvath

Library of Congress Cataloging-in-Publication Data

Boye, Robert
    Underwater paradise : the world's best diving
sites / by Robert Boye ; photographic coordination by Barbara Doernbach ; photographs by
Stephen Frink ... [et al.].
        p.   cm.
    ISBN 0—8109—1159—0
    1. Scuba diving—Guide-books.   I. Doern-
bach, Barbara.   II. Frink, Stephen.   III. Title.
GV840.S78B637   1989
797.2'3—dc19   89—250

Text © 1989 Robert Boye
Photographs © 1989 Robert Boye, Stephen Frink,
Paul Humann, Geri Murphy, Chris Newbert, Carl
Roessler, Marty Snyderman, Valerie Taylor, Paul
Tzimoulis

Published in 1989 by Harry N. Abrams, Incorporated,
New York. All rights reserved. No part of the contents
of this book may be reproduced without the written
permission of the publisher

A Times Mirror Company
Printed and bound in Italy

ACKNOWLEDGMENTS

WRITING is a solitary task. Writing a book about international diving is a complex undertaking involving travel, land accommodations, boats, equipment, and asking a lot of advice. We are grateful to the many companies and individuals who believed in the dream that became *Underwater Paradise* and in the dreamer who wrote it: Aggressor Fleet Ltd. (Wayne Hasson, Hal and Shirley Brown); Baja Expeditions Inc. (Tim Means and Gary Cotter); Dacor Corp. (Jim Foley); Dive Taveuni (Ric and Do Cammick); Divi Hotels (Peter Hughes); Henderson Aquatics, Inc. (Betsey Edmund); Ikelite Underwater Systems (Gale Livers); Marine Pacific Limited (Carl Bay); Nikonos Division of Nikon, Inc. (Frank Fennel); Seaward Holdings Ltd. (Lance Higgs); See & Sea Travel Service, Inc. (Carl Roessler); Trans Niugini Tours (Bob Bates); Rum Cay Club (David Melville). And along the way, numerous people contributed encouragement, colorful recollections, and good counsel: Peter Benchley, Tom Ettinger, Dinah and Bob Halstead, Alex Kerstitch, Jack McKenney, and Sandy Stewart.